FACILITY MANAGEMENT BRINGS WHAT

INTANGIBLE ADVANTAGES

JOHN LOK

Contents

Preface

Introduction

This book concerns how to apply how behavioral economic and psychological methods to attempt to explain whether your organization can be influenced to raise your employee individual productive efficiency as well as improve service performance to achieve to let your clients feel more satisfaction by effective human resource training or/and facility management methods. Can effective human resource training or/and facility management influences your organization's employee individual productive efficiency raising and/or service performance improving? Can effective workplace working environment facility management influence your organization's employee individual emotion and working attitude to be changed more positive to raise productive efficiency and/or service performance?

I shall apply psychological method to attempt to recommend whether it is the right time to your organization ought need to find methods to raise your organization's human resource trai8ning course(s) quality and/or improve your organization's facility management in-house service quality to let your employees feel more comfortable to work in your organization's any working environment in order to achieve the raising productive efficiency and/or improving service performance consequence in possible.

This book indicates whether organization's facility management in-house department or outsourced department can achieve to improve its office or warehouse working environment to be more comfortable to let employees to feel in order to influence their productive efficiencies to be raised or improving their service performance to bring customers' more satisfactory feeling.
I write this book aims to hope any organization leaders can attempt to apply psychological methods to predict whether their in-house

facility management service is enough or/and human resource management strategy and training course program strategies which both have relationship to influence their employees' productive efficiency and service performance in order to achieve aim to raise more satisfactory feeling to their customers. I believe that effective facility management can improve better workplace environment to influence employee individual productive efficiency raising as well as effective human resource training course program can improve employee individual service performance in order to achieve customers to feel more satisfactory service performance in consequence for the organization's service.

Whether do any organizations need facility management department? What function of benefits will bring when the organization sets up one facility management department? If the organization lacked one facility management department, what the disadvantage it will bring to influence the organization's operation? Does it has relationship between raising efficiency or improving performance and facility management department?

I shall indicate some evidences and causations to explain what will be occurred when the organization owns one facility management department or it lacks one facility management department in its organization. Any readers can make judgement whether in what situations , the organization needs to set up one facility management department in order to bring advantages or waste essential human resource or raise service cost from the facility management department.

Prologue

Table of contents

CHAPTER ONE

WHY FACILITY MANAGEMENT INFLUENCES PERFORMANCE

● Developing countries
facility management whether
need to be improved

Do developing countries need to facility management development to assist their businesses development, it is possible due to staff individual lacks knowledge to do whose job in whose organization ? What is the developing and developed countries' organizational human resource strategic difference, e.g. award strategies? I shall indicate one developing country,such as South Africa's businesses' general organizational human resource strategy case to explain whether what causes their human resource strategies, e.g. award managment strategies are different to compare developed countries, such as US, UK as well as I also indicate what weak points that they ought to concern in order to improve these developing countries' businesses productivities and efficienc, if South Africa 's firms hope to raise staff performance to be better. I shall explains that South Afria country governement needs to implement human resource development strategy as below:

In general, South Africa employers feel human resource development strategy is needed to innovate and attempt to ensure that they meet the needs of their economy. So, South Africa employers are considering whether how they ought need to improve their human resource strategies in their organizations in order to raise productive efficiencies and performance to their employees effectively. In fact, because South Africa country lacks effective human resource development to recommend to itself country's businessmen how to select the right employees to do right positions, how to evaluate whom has more effort to be promoted to do senior position, lacking fair reward and welfare to compensate to their employees. So, it brings many reasons to explain why in South Africa society unemployment and poverty still existence. Not all of the reaons have to do with the capabilities of people , may have to do with the unequal distribution of productive assets in South Africa society.

Nowadays, the South Africa employers only feel South Africa workers are only their own labour to use or sell. Hence, they won't like to provide reasonable and fair award to compensate for their Africa employees general lack high education level and skills. So, it also influences their award will not increase. Moreover, there are South Africans who have skilled labours to sell and they can not find buyers because there are not enough jobs , their skills do not match the demands, and there is a systematic process for information to flow between government, the workplace and labour.

Hence, many South African people are unemployed, due to their knowledge are not enough to satisfy or accept to employers' demands. It will cause South African income inequality will be continue serious. The salary range between the high education level and low education level of labours' difference is large. A cycle of income inequality, low skills and poor education have limited economic growth.

In fact, in South Africa society, many domestic people ae skilled agricultural and fishery workers, plant anf machine operators and assemblers, elementary occupational workers, non-permanent employees. They are low education level people. Otherwise, less doemstic people are legiclation, senior officials and managers, professionals, technicians and associate professionals , clerks, service are sales workers. So, the low educational level occupational domestic people must be kept low level to compare high educational level occupational people in South Africa society. However, the high education level occupational labour shortage is serious. Otherwise, the local low low educaional level labours number is excessive to supply in South Africa labour market. It causes the South Africa labour market supply and demand is inequal between the labour supply and employee demand number in society.

Thus, South Africa government has implemented whole country's human resource development strategy. It's key mission is to maximize the potential of the people of South Africa, though the acquisition of knowledge and skills to work productivity and competitively in order to achieve a rising quality of life for all, and implement an effective HR operational plan, together with the necessary HR need arrangement to satisfy every employer's labour need. The South Africa country HR development goals: To improve the human development and an improved basic social need for critical for a productive workforce and a successful economy, to reduce disparities in wealth and poverty, and develop a more unemployment society, to improve international confidence and investor perceptions of the economy. The actions include a basic foundation, consisting of early childhood development, general education at school, and adult education and training, securing skills, with the further and higher education and training bands to anticipate and respond to specific skill needs in society, participation in lifelong learning, an articulated demand to skills, generated by th eneeds of the public and private sectors, including those acquired for social development opportunities and the development of small business, implementing a research and innovation sector which supports industrial and employment growth policies. Hence, South Africa government is concerning itself country's young people's education policy, it ought plan how to innovate in order to improve HR development to satisfy employers' labour needs for long term economic benefits.

This new strategy therefore recognises both the demand and supply side HR issues, acknowledges that HRD is needed to implement from the foundations of early childhood development right through to labour market entry, recongizes systemic challenges as to successful HRD policy implementation, located HRD in the development issues , such as poverty, inequality, high unemployment levels. However, instead of develop countries feel HR development need. Most developed countries are also implementing a systematic strategy for HRD in support of economic growth and developments. They both feel need. It is perhaps due to the flexibility and capacity of workforce to adhust speedity and capacity of workforce in technology, production , trade and work organizations. Consequently, the ability to respond to these changes with speed and efficiency has more becaue the area where many countries seek a competitive advantage.

However, South Africa country feels it is very serious mismatch between the supply of and demand for skills in the South Africa labour market. So, it's HRD innovation main aim is to improve future itself country's society to reduce the mismatch problem to be serious between the supply of and demand for skills in the South Africa future labour market. So, such South Africa 's inequal supply and demand for human resources in labour market case, the South Africa government is implementing a high and intermediate level skills strategy on the supply side of high education level of labour to be provided in South Africa labour market as well as a demand strategy that is stimulated large-scale labour absorbing employment growth supported by a appropriate inputs of law-level skills training in order to satisfy future public or private organizations' labour demands.

Hence, higher education and training development will be South Africa future educational development trend in order to raise South Africa local high education knowledge level graduates number to be enough supplied to local labour market. It does not South Africa employers need to make decision to give high reward to attract overseas high educational level job competitors to go to South Africa to do any local employers' jobs. It may raise local South Africa graduates' competition in future Soutch Africa labor market. It will bring negative raising unemployment influence to South Africa high education level local graduates.

The developed countries , such as US, UK , they have high quality of educational enough institutions to provide local students to learn different kinds of subjects, e.g. law, accounting, engineering, science, chemical, architecture etc. different kinds of professional subjects. Thus, these developed countries can have enough universities and lecturers number to provide local students' learning needs in order to find any kinds of professional jobs in local labour market. Thus, the important difference between developed countries and developing countries' labour market is that developed countries' local high education level job applicants supply number is enough to satisfy local employers' high education level labour demand number. So, in general, the developed countries' reward is needed to compensate to graduated employees, the reward number can be lower level to compare developing countries' employers. Otherwise, developing countries' employees feel difficult to find the righ high education level job applicants to fill high education level positions , due to local graduates number doe snot enough to supply to developing countries' labour market to let employers to select whom is the most right applicants. So, they need to raise general local normal reward level to attract overseas high graduation level professions to let they can select who are the high quality applicants to work in their organizations more easily. It seems that if developing countries, such as South Africa's government can raise enough universities, high schools, primary school students number and it can train many teachers to raise their teaching effort in order to raise future new yough generation's education level. Then, when these developing countries have enough high education level graduate number to be supplied to local labour market to let themselve countries' employers to select whom is the most right job applicants in order to achieve to employ the local graduate students intention.

When any developing countries' employers choose to employ the local graduate students to fill their high educational level positions in preference. Then, their reward must not raise in order to attract overseas educational level graduate students intention. However, if developing country, such as South Africa government hopes to have enough graduate students to be supplied to local labour market. It needs to find methods how to raise teachers' teaching effort in primary, secondary and high schools in order to train them to own enough teaching effort to teach next young generation's learning need. Then, their developing countries; high -educational level graduate students number will be raised to supply in local labour markets. It will bring benefits to local employers who can reduce wage/salary to reward overseas job applicants (staffs cost reducing benefits) to bring economic development benefit when it avoids local businesses' failure risk, due to they have no enough expenditure to employ many overseas high educational level employees to fill their organizations any high education level positons in long term.

In conclusion, developing countries' human resource development needs to be improved or revised, if there are many employers feel need to pay very high salaries to attract and select overseas high education level job applicants to fill their organizations' any high educational level positions. However, local high education development must need to revise in order to help many local students have chance to enter schools to learn to earn high education level knowledge to prepare to do any domestic employers; high education level jobs in themselves organizations. Then they will not need to raise high salary level to compensate rewards to their countries themselves local graduate students, when themselves countries have excessive high educational level graduate student applicants number supplies to domestic labour market to let local employer to choose.

● The relationship between facility management and raising employee individual productive performance efficiency

There are one considering question to any business leaders: Does organization need to set up facility management to assist them to raise themselves employee individual productive performance efficiency in order to satisfy client attitude to their performance needs as well as their managers' work efficient needs? It is one very important question to be worth to any organizations' considerations. Because if the organization's human resource department can not achieve it's aim to raise employee individual efficient aim or raise product number productive aim or improve service performance aim to let their customers or managers to earn positive emotion feedback. Then, it seems that the organization's human resource department can not bring valued attribution to let its organization to earn long term economic or non-economic positive benefits from its overall employees' performance in its organizations. So, it means that it doe not need to set up one human resource department to assist the ineffective organization's human resource department. It is one non-essential effective department to the ineffective organization, even it is wasting time and management's nervous and effort and resource to develop its internal human resource department to be grown up. Thus, it also brings this question: Does it essential to set up one human resource department in any small, medium, large organizations? I shall give some useful cases and assumptions to describe whether what factors will have possible to influence employee individual efficiency or productive performance to any organizations when they have one human resource department or have no one human resource department in their organizations.

Firstly, I assume the organization's one facility management department can bring some related human resource issue related benefits or causes any one of below factors as well as the organization's human resource department can cause any one of these factors to bring any one below of human resource issue related benefits to the organization when the organization had set up one in house human resource department in its organization. Then, any one of these factors can bring benefits, such as the raising productive efficiency or the improving service performance or the raising productive number etc. different human resource related benefits to the organization.

Jean, W (et al.) (pp64-65,2004) stated one case study , it concerns both organizations of Quarriers and Richmond fellowship Scotland (RFS), they have grown rapidly and diversified since the mid-1990s. For example, they are increasingly delivering services, such as support for people with learning disabilities within individual's communities rather than in large scale residential projects, key informants in both organizations felt that the organizations were now at a critical point in their organizational life cycles. However, they indicated these both organizations were encountering challenges: retaining their cutting edge innovation, when controlling the level of bureaucracy that accompanies growth. At the time of this research RFS employed around seven hundred 700 staff and Quarriers nearly one thousand 1,000. Both organizations have well –developed HRD strategies and practices, (including supervision), are recognized as investors in people and providing training for managers as developers. They also aspire to be learning organizations. It seems that both organizations therefore provided appropriate working environments to explore the development behaviors of line managers.

It seems that it can explain that these both mental health service organizations had set up one human resource department, it can provide effective HRD, including raising supervision skill to mental health service managers . So, the both organizations' training department can provide any useful supervising training skill courses for managers as developers to learn how to supervise their departments to raise themselves mental health service teams' efficiencies and service performance to their mental patients. Hence, their different mental health department service managers can be trained to raise excellent supervisory skills to manage and arrange their team members how to work efficiently in order to raise excellent service performance and provide high quality services continue to be delivered in respect of individuals with mental health difficulties or learning disability. These both organizations stress the values of human-centered approaches implicit in the social care model of care. Their mission statements aim to ensure the best possible high quality services continue to be delivered in respect of individuals with mental health difficulties or learning disability. This aims to meet these individual's right aspirations and needs as well as to work together to overcome personal and social disadvantages, inspire optimism , create opportunity and offer choice to children, families and others in need of support. When, these both mental health service organizations have a clear aims, then their human resource department can know what their service needs and review their mental patients' complaints in order to find what their mental health care service needs to be improved to let every mental health service managers to know and learn from its training courses more easily. So, when they know what are their aims, then their trainers can know how to teach supervision skill to let their mental care managers know they ought how to supervise their team members to work in order to raise raising service performance efficiency to serve their mental patients more easily.

Thus, due to these two mental health care service organizations had set up one effective human resource department, its in –house training courses can provide excellent training service to teach the mental health service leaders knowledge and train their mental health care skills how to let they to know how to teach their every team different kinds of mental health care workers to learn their knowledge as well as provide effective supervision to manage them how to allocate their time to serve every mental child or family patients in order to cure every one's mental illness effectively in short time. Thus, these two both mental health service organizations had made right decision to set up one human resource department to provide in-house supervision training service in order to implement one effective supervisory strategy to let their mental health care service mangers to learn how to supervise their mental health care service workers to work effectively in order to let their mental patients to believe their mental illness to be cured satisfactorily. It seems effective supervisory is one important factor to bring these two mental healthcare service organizations' leading efforts to be obvious raised effectively. It implies that the HRD department is real need to these both mental health service organizations. If they had not designed or set up this human resource department to arrange how to provide in-house supervisory training courses to train their mental health care service managers to learn how to supervise their mental care service workers efficiently and effectively. It is possible that their mental health mangers (leaders) can not be trained to own excellent leading or supervisory efforts to supervise or lead their every team's mental health care service workers or members to serve their mental patients to let them to feel they have efforts to cure their mental illnesses satisfactory. So, the HRD is critical influential factor to arrange effective supervisory training courses to raise every mental health care mangers' supervisory effort in order to raise their mental health care service performance to bring their every team to serve their mental patients to let they feel they can provide good mental care service to cure their mental illnesses satisfactory. Hence, the consequence of the raising performance of mental health service workers, it has relationship between the HRD and the effective training supervisory factor.

Leslie, W. Rus et. al (pp.62-63 2007) stated Frederick Herzberg has developed an approach to motivation that has gained acceptance in management. They explained that his theory is referred to by several names: motivation-maintenance approach, dual-factor approach, and motivator-hygiene approach. Herzberg's approach deals primary with motivation through job design. The approach is based on the belief that the factors that demotivate employees are different from the factors the motivate employees.

Herzberg maintains that the factors usually associated with the work environment. These factors include much things as job status, interpersonal relations with supervisors and peers, the style of supervision that the person receives company policy and administration, job security, working conditions, pays and aspects of personal life that are affected by the work situation.

Hence, he believed that raising employee individual performance , it includes these both factors. The first is hygiene factor, relates to the working environment. It includes policies and administration, style of supervision , working conditions, inter-personal relations, factors that affect employee's personal life, salary /wage status, job security feeling. The another factor is motivator factor, related to the job itself. It includes achievement, recognition, challenging work, increased responsibility, promotion or senior position advancement, personal growth. Hence, the author feels that external working environment and the job itself to the employer personal satisfactory feeling these both factors will influence how the employee individual performance to be motivated or demotivated to influence how he/she like to put how much whose effort to be performed to finish or achieve whose every task either inefficient or efficient performance. Thus, the author felt what factors can influence employees' performance to be raised or weakened. They include job stress, motivation and communication enable them to be compared to the another working environment factor., they have more influential effort to influence employee individual performance to be raised or weakened more easily. Also, he felt the job itself satisfactory feeling factor to the employee and the organization's working environment factor both must have relationship to influence any employee individual performance to be raised or weakened.

The job stress can influence employee individual performance. Job stress is produced when one can't properly coordinate available resources and job demands with personal abilities. Job stress is derived from a situation of job environment to threat to an individual. Hence , if the employee often feels difficult to work in a job stress working environment. Then, it will influence her/her performance to be weakened. Thus, employers ought need to consider how to avoid any employees feel job stress to influence whose performance in their organizations. Human resource department staff relation manger can attempt to enquiry every feeling job stress of employee when he/she begins feel job stress and he ought attempt to help them to find where the causing of job stress sources are coming from external environment factors (non organizational factor, e.g. themselves mental illness or his/her unsatisfactory salary or welfare feeling to whose employer or internal organizational factor, e.g. unreasonable policy, noise and danger working environment in order to solve their negative emotion to avoid job stress causes poor performance.

Another factor is motivation to influence employee individual performance, it is defined as the willingness or desire to do something, conditioned by the activity of the ability to satisfy some needs, such as the employee needs to finish the task in order to earn higher wage/salary or promotion chance or performance appreciation. So, it seems today enterprises' HRD needs to find methods how to realized that actions of motivating their employees are crucial in order to achieve the organizations' raising efficiency or productive performance or raising profit etc. different goals.

The motivated employees relate to the manners of self satisfaction, sell-fulfillment and commitment that are expected produce better quality of work. So, it seems that motivation has relationship to influence employee performance, one demotivated employee won't raise employee performance. Otherwise, one motivated employee will raise employee performance. Hence HRD needs to provide training to let the managers have chance to have been asked to know the feedback gained from the employees which probably affects their work motivation. For right time of delivering such information, this they may perform based on the messages they receive. In obtaining such as good performance, the managers must show the initiatives of developing and providing opportunities to learn new skills to their employees through the communication process. Thus, such as enhancing training and non-traditional compensation , e.g. pay for skill, bonuses, gain sharing, and profit sharing, which will affect job quality. Thus, intangible factor, such as improving workplace environment and job itself quality both factors can influence employee individual working performance, instead of tangible factor, such as raising salary level, promotion or appreciation change. These both factors can make incentive in ways that reward quality and performance improvement to frontline or back office workers, instead of increasing earnings may be significant greater factor to increase motivation and productivity. The intangible factor, e.g. redesigning of the job itself often involving both new information technology and increasing worker autonomy was resulting increase in efficiency or redesigning new method to avoid the employee to feel increased task complexity, responsibility, autonomy , training and gain sharing are interdependent and mutually reinforcing. For example, it may be far more effective both to train frontline employees in problem –solving and to permit them to solve more problems than to make either change alone. Thus, it seems that more chance to promote or appreciate or higher wages encouragement which are not the main factors to influence the employee to raise performance. Because some employees will feel bore or difficult to do the job, so how to redesign the job itself to be better or more attractive or how to reduce the employee's job stress is caused by the unhappily or feeling high dangerous working environment risk or noise or dispute with difficult cooperation relation to staffs will cause poor or negative emotion to the employee , then which will be other main factor to influence the employee individual performance to be weakened or poor in the organization.

However, sometimes intangible factor, e.g. job stress , boredom, promotion chance, appreciation will have more influential to the employee individual working behavior to be better or worse more than tangible factor, e.g. raising salary/wage level , increasing welfare provision , e.g. increasing holiday days, free lunch allowance, cheap air ticket allowance, son or daughter student education allowance etc. Psychological factor is more important to influence how the employee performs in the organization.

The another raising employee performance factor is performance evaluation measurement plan. It has close relationship to raise employee individual efficiency and organizational effectiveness. HRD needs have an effective strategic plan or performance evaluation plan to measure effectiveness and efficiency for every employee performance measures, the performance evaluation plan can bring these advantages to the organization , e.g. making more accurate decision whether the employee is value to be promotes to do the senior position. Efficiency is oriented towards successful input transformation into outputs, where effectiveness measures how outputs interact with the economic and social environment. Thus, HRD needs to find how and why what causes the employee work inefficiency or under (below level) productive performance in order to improve her/his performance to achieve the organization's minimum performance acceptable level. For example, how to upgrade the low talent or foolish employee job related knowledge or skill to be better or improved when he/she feels difficult to finish the job.

In effectiveness vs. efficiency view point, there are various opinions regarding valuation of any organizations. However, Chavan , M. (2009) states Frey etc. al (2009) had found the findings that efficiency information provides different data compared to effectiveness one. So the chain of effects: From efficiency information (input is the first step causes the process step), then the second process step brings the causation or consequent step , such as effective information (output causes the outcome final step). It is the chain of effects process. It explained that effectiveness oriented companies are concerned with output, sales, quality, creation of value added, innovation , cost reduction. It measures the degree to which a business achieves its goals or the way output, interact the economic and social environment. So, in the workplace may take various forms, such as relationship between leader and staff, employee's personal attitude with the organization, involvement in the decision making process, psychological feeling. So, it is possible that the causing supervisor performance is caused by the staff personal attitude towards the organization. Thus, organization needs to consider how to change the employee individual attitude when it occurs the employee the negative emotion or attitude to work in its organization.

So, it seems the effectiveness vs. efficiency measurement strategy, such as hoe to measure efficiency between inputs and outputs or how successfully the inputs have been transformed into inputs, e.g. how to stable production, avoiding defects, reduced speed, minor, stoppages, set up and adjustment equipment failure. etc. issues which can influence employee individual attitude to be caused positive or negative emotion to work in whose organization. Employers can not neglect all these above issues because they will be possible to influence employee attitude to work efficiently or effectively. These input elements can bring either positive or negative output effort in either inefficient or efficient way. Thus, HRD needs to consider how to improve output efforts in order to raise efficiency or efficient performance to its employees. It seems that efficiency and effective measurement strategic plan factor will influence employees performance how performs in whose organizations. Hence, manpower performance can be increased by putting efforts to factors that enhance the employees' motivational level, creativity, job satisfaction and comfort workplace environment etc. intangible factors influence.

Why does HRM department designing has relationship to raise employee performance? HRM can be defined as the process of analyzing and managing an organization's human resource needs to ensure satisfaction of its strategic objectives. It is a pattern of planned HR development an activities which affect the behavior of individuals with the intention of enabling organizations to achieve their goals. So, it seems that all HR activities are dependent upon the manager's efforts to formulate and implement the organization strategy as well as it has direct relationship for resulting and developing their employees as well as their behavior, attitudes, brings indirect relationship how to influence and performance to achieve the organization's goals.

Thus, it brings this question: Why and how HRM can influence employee performance? We need to know employee performance is explained with quantity of output, quality of output , timeliness of output, presence attendance on the job, efficiency of the work completed and effectiveness of work completed. Hence, employee performance is the successful completion of tasks by a selected individual or individuals (team), it is measured by a supervisor or organization to pre-defined acceptable standards when efficiently and effectively utilizing available resource within a changing environment. In fact, performance is about behavior or what employees produce or the outcomes of their work. However, HRD needs have these duties, and duties can influence how employee performs, such as competitive compensation level, training and development, performance appraisal, recruitment package and maintaining morale. So, management ought need to consider how to design HRD these tasks duties or functions issues, what factors will influence how employees choose or decide to perform their behaviors to do their tasks in organizations. It seems that how to design or arrange HRD 's functions which will influence how employee individual performs to do whose tasks daily. Thus, if the organization can design its HRD has effective functions, then it will influence its employees to do more effective performance or better or improved behavioral performance in their organizations. Otherwise, ineffective HRD functions, it will influence how every employee decides or chooses to do ineffective behavioral performance or inefficient productive behaviors easily in their organizations. So, any organizations need to concern how to design their HRD's functions to be useful in order to achieve more effective consequence.

Finally, I states the tourism service industry case to attempt explanation why and how HRD is needed to set up in order to raise service performance in this service industry's organizations. How to raise tourism industry service performance? For tourism industry example, this service industry will combine with many other industries, such as food and beverage, transportation, sightseeing, health and beauty and hotel industry. However, all these industries are service nature provision, e.g. how to increasingly improve in the hotel management, service quality and work efficiency in order to increase the customers' level of satisfaction. The superior service performance issues will be the important factor to influence whole tourism industry and related tourism industries client numbers to be raised, e.g. modern international attractive airport can attract overseas travelers to visit the country's airport for their aim instead of travelling aim, beautiful sea port design and high class hotels and restaurants design, offering the best location, best service and food to let travelers to feel. So, the country's hotels themselves service quality need to be improved to attract many overseas travelers to select to visit the country when they need to live in the country's any hotels anyway, they are first time to visit this country or repeat visit to this country.

Thus, when one country's any related tourism industry's service level is unsatisfactory to let it travelers to feel, then it will bring negative influence to them to choose to travel this country again. For hotel case example, how to excite the country's hotels employees' performance raising? In fact, the work performance of hotel employee is to important that the success of the hotel may depend on it highly satisfied employee will produce high quality of service and results in highly satisfied customers.

I believe that how to teach hotel frontline employees to use of equipment, e.g. how to improve coffee making frontline service staffs, how to use coffee machine to coffee making knowledge, skill and positive attitude to serve the hotel clients when they have needs to buy coffee to drink in the hotel. So, the frontline hotel coffee service staffs need to be trained to apply the coffee machine how to make good taste coffee to let hotel guest to drink, or how to train the hotel frontline room booking service staffs' skill to operate the computer system to help any hotel guests to book any rooms to live or check who is the pre hotel room booking guests to avoid them to waste time to wait their rooms to live. So, the hotel training courses need have good trainers to teach any departments how to learn hotel computer system to be operated in efficient proficiency way. Because many hotel guests do not like to waste time to wait their service when they feel need to find their help. They hope that they can serve them immediately.

The another factor is that hoe to let hotel frontline staffs to feel job satisfaction , it means that how the employee feels joy and happiness result from doing the job descriptions, such as joy to work with the co-workers, satisfy with the income and rewards from doing the job or good attitude towards the job, satisfaction is good attitude towards work, value of work, challenge od work , freedom of is the feeling of the work which is like or not like in the areas of job description, compensation, rewards benefits, relationship with others in the organization, such as hotel. So, hotel needs have good reward plan, performance evaluation method, job designing strategy, promotion chance in order to encourage every hotel staff to work efficiency in whose departments.

The final factor to influence hotel employee personal working performance, it is work motivation, work motivation means something in a person to motivate them to work, to move and finish any task within the goal. Work motivation means the ability to motivate a person to work hard to achieve the objective of the work of the organization within his / her volunteer of without force. Work motivation is important tool to positively push the employee to love their work, willing to work hard to finish the task with high quality and work hard to achieve the high level of effectiveness and efficiency.

In tourism industry, airline service and travel agent which are the prior contact travelling service providers to travelers. So, the airline attendant service will influence the travelers' choices to find the travel agent or another travel agent to buy air tickets to catch the airline's air plan or another airline. For airline service attendant performance case example, airlines feel airline attendant age will influence every service performance. Why does airlines do not permit their frontline airline passenger attendant individual age can not above 50 age or between 45 to 50 age? The reason is simple, because airline frontline passenger service attendants, they need often fly to different countries, but their working time must not fix, they have no stable working hours and time to fly. They sometime need to catch air plans in continue several nights, then they will be possible to sleep one night to continue next morning flying or night flying. Even, they have no one day sleep, they only have more than three hours or less than three hours to sleep in busy seasonal travelling periods. Hence, they will have no enough nervous to serve their airline passengers in possible. In long term lacking enough nervous air plane working environment, it will possible to influence their performance to serve their air plane passengers to be poor in possible. Thus, it explains why airlines usually do not permit their frontline airline attendants to prolong their service period to serve their airline passengers on air planes. Because airlines usually assume that they must lack enough nervous to serve their airline passengers when they need often fly overnight flying planes to arrive different countries in their frontline airline attendant career.

However, many airlines do not plan to encourage them to leave their airline career early. They will choose to change their positions in house training department. So, they have enough airline passenger service working experience, they can attribute their airline passenger service knowledge to teach the junior airline attendants how they ought serve their airline passengers to let them to feel more service satisfactory feeling form their performance on air planes. SO, these airlines won't lose these old age talent airline attendant employees. Their passenger service experience can assist the new young age airline attendants to learn that whether how they do the best decision to deal any passenger complaint or sudden accident occurrence in any sudden difficult predictive flying environment in order to protect their passengers' safety or solve their reasonable or unreasonable complaints more easily. Even , if the new young age airline passenger attendant can perform very excellent to let any passengers to appreciate often. Then, the old age attendant trainer and the young age attendant both will have chance to be promoted to senior position level or raising their salary level fairly, when the HRD training department believe the excellent performance airline attendant is taught from the old age airline attendant trainer. SO, how to design the training courses quality which will have direct to influence the attendant trainers to teach their trainees to be better or worse.

IN conclusion, effective HRD designing functions will bring long term economic and non-economic related benefits to raise service performance. Otherwise, ineffective HRD designing functions will not bring long term economic and non-economic related benefits to raise service performance in possible in any organizations.

Reference

Chavan, M. (2009) The balanced scorecard: a new challenge// Journal of management development. Vol. 28, issue 5, pp. 393-406. www. Emerald insight.com/0262.17111.htm < ziureta2011.02.24>

Jean, W. & Monica Lee & Jim Stewart (2004). Routledge Studies In Human Resource Development: London and New York. Routledge publish, pp. 64-65.

Leslie, W, Rus & Lloyd, L, Byars (2007), Supervision: Key Link To Productivity: America, The Mc-Graw-Hill companies Inc. pp. 62-63.

Source: adopted from Frey and Widmer (2009)

● facility managment assists organizational development

When on firm sets up one facility management department, whether it can assist itself organization to implement change management strategy more easily? What is change management mean? Change management is a critical part of any project that leads, manages, and enables people to accept new processes, technologies, systems, structures and values.

It is the activities that helps staffs to adapt good change management from present way of working to the desired way of working. So, change management is the continuous process of operation an organization with its marketplace in order to achieve more responsively and effectively than competitors.

In fact, any organization's change, it must strat with a vision. Anyway its changing need is from external environment factors influence, e.g. economic, social or technological or internal factors, e.g. policy, systems or structure , creating a vision wil clarify the direction for the change. In addition, the vision will assist in motivating those that are impacted to take action in the right direction. So it ensures that vision can assist change management more easily. However, whether human resource department strategy can follow the organization's vision to assist change management to implement more easily, when the organization feels need to change.

In fact, a strategy(HR) will ensure the vision is achieved more easily when the organization needs to change, it can provide direction for achieving the vision when its organization needs to change. Without a strategic plan and vision, the change effort will not be successful easily. Hence, when the organization decides to change, it also neds to change HR strategy, e.g. how to match the best employee to change his/her old position to do the right new position from company's internal staffs choices when it needs to change , how to redesign reard o compensate new staffs when they replace the old staffs to do the the old staffs' positions. It seems that HR strategy will need to change, when the organization needs to change its internal organizational structure.

However, the HR department needs to implement how to change some issues related to human resource matters, such as solving these HR problem when the organization needs to change, e.g. employee resistance, solving different communication breakdown, insufficient time devoted to training, reducing staff turnover during the organizational changing period, reduced costs exceeded budget. The change obstacles of employee resistance include solving the staffs relationship with the different department leaders' team to satisfy employee concerns on s personal acceptable level, asking for their feedback and responding to their concerns honestly and openly. The communication breakdown obstacles include communicating key information to employees on an on-going and consistent basis. Staff turnover obstacles include engaging the leader's team by involving them in the initiative, coaching, mentor and enriching their new roles.

Thus, HRD needs to particular the organizational change tasks, such as needs to know what the changes, their impact, rationale and benefits are, it needs to explain them to anyone to believe the chane in worthwhile, how th change is impacting the old staff individual existing workload, or it needs to communicate the need for change to explain the first steps, how the changing position staffs need to be supported and when they have achieved quick to gain benefits to themselves, it needs to explain how the changes impact the same group, what changes will happen and when, explaining the change leaders what know their responsibilities and the commitment expectations to their team memebers, describing what change has successfully occurred in these groups in the past, explaining how and why these changing staff can learn from what work did or did not well.

Hence, in the whole changing steps, HRD needs to participate every team through each stage of the change effort. The step one, it needs to assist organization to change urgent message to let staffs to know. The step two, it needs to buid a guiding team to help departmental staffs to adapt to changing tasks more easily. The step three, it needs to choose the right vision to give right direction to let organizational change method is implemented in a correct way. The step four, ot needs to commicate every for one-by-one to do empower action clearly, the need of help of changing staffs to create short -term wins in every changing process. Moreover, the HRD needs to consider thee matters do not work, such as focusing on building a rational business case, getting top management, approval, and ignoring all feeling, that are blocking change, ignoring a lack of urgency and immediately to create a vision and strategy. The HRD can not misunderstand the difficulty of driving people from their comfort zones. Hence, it needs have enough staffs number to already to replace the low skillful of employees when they can not adapt change to do the new tasks. Then, they will need have highly attractive people to be chosen to replace them to do the new changing of natural characteristic task to satisfy different department's needs after organization had changed its internal structure. Thus, HRD has responsibility to arrange enough staffs number and explains what the new changing tasks to let the changing task need of employees to know whether they ought how to do in order to adapt to do new changing of tasks more easily. Hence, it seems that HRD can assist organizatonal development when it decides to implement changing strategy in the organizational restructure changing period.

- facility management department assists management strategic development

Does facility management assist training strategic arrangement more easily? When one large organization needs to spend too much expenditure for facility management to raise training and development. If it had not set up one facility management department to let employees to feel comfortable to sit in training room to enjoy training and learning feeling in the training room , it will be possible to implement poor trainings to cause failed training. Hence, if one HRD could help every different knids of training course to focus on issues, such as training methods, selecting the most right trainer to teach different training courses, program design and following trainee characteristics to choose the most right training courses to let them to learn. Then, it will be more easier to implement every training chouse to let trainees to learn successfully.

In fact, when one organization has none one facility management department to keep training room can have good learning environment to provide training learning service to let employees feel comfortable to learn , it will bring high change of training failure and raise training cost and poor performance. So, it seems that training failure has relationship with poor HRD and good training room learning environment, include: unskilled practitioner provides invalid training , skilled practitioner provides invalid training or valid training but learning does not transfer of valid training, learning transfer , but hierarchical level, organizational (dominant) is too much limited to grow up its human resource department to develop, lacking effective characteristics of human resource development, e.g. poor performance appraise standards, restricted standardized training.

All of these above issues will have relationship to HRD. HRD includes psychology, sociology, managment and adult education. This is not a comprehensive review of related to training effectiveness, HRD and organizatonal culture, but is intended to be representatives. HRD needs to know there is no single measure of training success, such as productivity or job satisfaction. There are numerous qualitative and quantitative evaluation, approaches useful in determining training effectiveness.

However, successful training depends on the benefits of various groups including: organizational leaders, supervisors, trainees, HRD managers and training facilitators. So, organizations need have one good HRD plan (human resource development) plan in order to train every training teachers to provide effective training courses to let every trainee to learn in order to apply to work to raise efficiency or improve performance successfully. So, HRD is important to influence every training whether it is successful or failure training course.

Thus, any large organization needs have one effective facility management strategy to keep confortable learning and training environment in order to provide enough number of excellent training teachers (trainers) to assist its different departments to provide useful training courses to let every trainee to learn. Every trainer individual knowledge, skill, working experience will help his/her organization to train the new employment staff to learn their knowledge, skill effectively. So,, it seems that one effective HR department can assist its organization to develop HR (trainers) to be excellent training teachers to teach their traineers (new employment staffs) to absord their knowledge, skill to prepare to do their new position more to avoid none training cost waste successfully.

● facility management department assists
diversity in the workplace to be benefits

Nowadays, globalization requires more interaction among people from diverse background. So, large organizations will need to consider when they have need to develop overseas markets. Their offices will have different countries' staffs to cooperate to work together. For this reason, profit and non-profit organizations need to become more diversified to remain competition. Maximizing and capitalizing on workplace diversity is an important issue for management. It brings this question: Can human resource department assist the organization's diversity development in order to let continue people to cooperate to work in order to raise performance or productivity or efficieny easily. For example, if the organization's HRD is effective, the interviewers can ensure to help their organizations to select whether what countriess' applicant whom is the most right applicant to do the departmental tasks, one China company's finance department needs one applicant who familizes US accounting/finance policy knowledge and owns US related finance and accountinr working experience to do this fiance manager position. Then, the China fiem needs to decide whether it ought to select the foreign US country's domestic applicant who owns many years of finance and accounting working experience and US accounting/finance university subject knowledge to do this finance manager position or select itself country's China domestic applicant who owns US finance/accounting related working experience and familizes US accounting/finance subjects knowledge. Although, if the China company selected the local applicant who owns finance/accounting knowledge and US company finance/accounting related working experience to do this finance manager positin. The advantages are that the finance manager and whose finance team staffs who can speak fluent chinese language. So, the finance manager and his/her finance department staffs can communicate to bring easier cooperation. But, it does not guarantee that he/she must lead or supervise his/her finance deparment staffs to raise peformance or efficiency daily.

Otherwise, if the China firm select one foreign US applicant to do this finance manager position. Although, this US foreign finance manager can not speak fluent Chinese languare and he/she can only speaks American language. It is possible that the finance department staffs who all are Chinese. They can not understand English language easier. It is possible to bring communication difficult problem between the US foreign finance manager and his/her finance department staffs. But, the US foreign finance manager who has competitive effort is that his/her local US finance/accounting related working experience and university graduation of finance/accounting subject knowledge is better to compare to all China applicants whose own similar accounting/finance knowlege and related working experience in China. It seems that the foreign US finance manager applicant can perform more excellent to compare all China domestic finance manager applicants. If the finance manager's duty needs to familiarize US acocunting/finance policy to calculate tax and profit for US government tax department , due to this firm needs to sell products to US market often. It is possible that the foreign US finance manager applicant can lead or supervise whose finance department staffs to raise efficiency to work more easily, due to his/her familiar US accounting/finance policy and working experience is useful more than the China local applicants who owns more China accounting/finance knowledge and China accounting/finance related working experience.

Due to this finance manager position needs the applicant must own many years US firm accounting/finance working years and US education is prefer. Hence, HRD needs to consider diversity of workplace problem when it decides to employ one US foreign applicant to do this finance manager position to replace China local applicant to supervise or lead all Chinese staffs to work in finance department. So, knowing how to supervise finance staffs to cooperate to work efficiently and raise performance which will be the applicant's strength to do this position to the US applicant. However, the US foreign finance manager' s language and culture , education level, related finance and accounting working experience must be different to all Chinese finance staffs. Hence, workplace diversity issue will be this organization's HRD which needs to concern hoe to let different Chinese finance staffs and the American finance manager to easier adapt to work together in this company's finance department.

The best method is that this company's HRD needs to employ both Chinese and American people who can cooperate to work in human resource department together. The advantage is that when this company's HRD has these two countries' people to work, they can apply themselve countries' HR working experience and HR management knowledge to choose the most right applicants to do the positions, e.g. the finance deparment needs one finance manager, the US HRD manager can give better recommendation to know how to choose the best US finance manager. So, international organizations need have one effective facility management department to keep all working environment to the best to let different countries staffs to work together in their companies. Then, their performance will raise more easily.

Hence, in any diversity organizations, supervisors and managers need recognize the ways in which the workplace is changing. Managing diversity is significant organizational challenge. So, the diversity organizations' HRD needs to select the applicants who own more different countries' working experience and managerial skills in order to adapt to accommodate a multicultural working environment. The department manager applicants need have different countries effectively manage diverse workforces. It provides a general definition for workforce diversity, discusses the benefits and challenges of managing diverse workplace, and presents effective strateges for managing diverse workforce. Moreover, the diverse organization's HRD needs have effective performance evaluation strategy to review manager individual management practices and develop new and creative approaches to managing people. They aims to bring positive changes will increase work performance and customers service to let their organization can develop in diverse organizational working environment.

Why does diversity in the workplace need to occur to satisfy future some organizations' needs? Significant changes in the workplace have occurred , due to downsizing and outsourcing, which has greatly affected the organization's human resource management needs to be changed also. For example, globalization and new technologies have changed workplace practices, and there has been a trend toward longer working hours. Generaly speaking, organizational restructuring usually results, in fewer people doing more work. So, some organizations' HRD needs to select the efficient workers to continue to serve their departments.
When they need to discuss the non-efficient or below productive workers, again recruiting the new efficient working applicants to replace them. It is future organizational restructuring tend. So, any organization's HRD needs to concern how to devise to keep the most efficient workers to continue to serve for their organizational departments and how to select the most efficient applicants to do the jobs after the organization restructures.

What benefits of diversity in the workplace are bought to the diverse organizations? Diversity is beneficial to both employees and employers. Although, employees are interdependent in the workplace, respecting individual differences can increase productivity. Diversity in the workplace can reduce lawsuits and increase marketing opportunities, e.g. foreign sale market development, recruitment of the most right overseas applicants to do the jobs which need overseas educational learning knowledge and overseas working experiene, creating and building good business image to overseas market. When flexibility and creativity are keys to competitiveness, diversity is critical for a organization's sussess. Also, the consequences of loss of time and money should avoid.

Hence, future department managers need to own managing a diverse work population working experience when their organizations are international. Training department also needs to provide training courses to train new employing managers to learn how to deal more simply acknowledging differences in people. It involves learn how to teach every team's staffs to accept recognizing the value of differences, learn how to deal combating discrimination, and learn how to make reasonable decision to select whom can be the right staff to be promote as well as learn how to deal complaints an dlegal action against the organization. Due to different countries people work together to non necessary cause argument.

However, HRD and department managers need to know negative attitudes and behaviors can be barrier to organizational diversity because they can harm working relationships and damage morale and work productivity. Negative attitudes and behaviors in the workplace include: prejudice, discrimination, which should never be needed by management for hiring and termination practices, it can lead to raise organizational cost in long term , because the organization will have many overseas staffs choose to resign, if they felt discrimination is serious. Then these organizations will have lost any talent overseas staffs , due to their designation, any team efficiency will reduce, even performance will be poor when any team lacks talent overseas or different countries staffs and itself local staffs to work together. Hence, management level to staffs, e.g. supervisors, managers need to be trained to learn how to avoid to bring negative attitudes and behaviors to let overseas foreign countries staffs to feel unhappu to work together.

Training needs to be provides to train managers to be effective and are aware that certain skills are necessary for creating a successful , diverse workforce . For example, managers must understand discrimination and its consequences. Also, managers must recognize their own cultural biases and prejudices. Diversity is not about differences among groups, but rather about differences among individuals. Each individual is unique and does not repesent or speak for a particular group. Even, managers also need be willing to change organization of necessary. HRD also needs to provide training to let organization leaders , e.g. The lacking overseas working experience of CEO needs to learn how to manage diversity in the workplace to be successful in the future. So, training needs concentrate on teaching high, middle and low management level staffs' managerial skill how to corporate with different countries' staffs or lead or supervise them to work efficiently, happily, unfortuately. It is not easy to train these management skill to them. It mainly depends on the manager's ability to understand what is best for the organization based on teamwork and the dynamic of the workplace.

In fact, managing diversity is a process for creating a work environment that everyone. When creating a successful diverse workplace, an effective manager should focus on personal awareness. Both managers and team members need to be aware of their personal biases. These organizations need to develop , implement and maintain ongoing training because a one day session of traing won't change people's behavior. Managers need to concern these issues in diversity working environment: social gatherings and business neetings,where every member must listen adn have the chance to speak, are good ways to create happy working environment, managers need implement policies, such as mentoring programs to provide different countries staffs access to information and opportunities.

In conclusion, HRD needs to concern how to let a diverse workforce environment to implement effectively, how to let diverse work teams bring high value to organizations, how to let individual difference to bring benefit the workplace by creating a competitive effort and increasing work productivity, how to lead or train diversity management benefits every team by creating a fair and safe workplace environment where everyone has access to opportunities and challenges. Finally, HRD will need to train management leve staffs, e.g. supervisor, manager, CEO in a diverse workforce, it should be used to to educate every team members about diversity and its issues, including organization policies and regulations. Most workplaces are made up of diverse cultures, so organizations need to learn how to adapt to be successful. This is important successful factor to a diverse organization.

● Effective facility management department characteristics

What is the strengths and weaknesses between owning human resource organization and lacking facility management organization? How to achieve more effective human resource department development on organizational raising productivity? In fact, effective human resource development and facility management strategy can enhance productivity in order to reduce poor performance in organization in long time. For example: enhancing the efficiency of human resource training to train many excellent performance staffs aim from the human resource training function. It brings this question: Whaat factors determine and identify to affect human resource development and organizational productivity and changing positive attitude of the senior management to raise their managerial efforts successfully?

Human resource development is the engagement of people to work in order to achieve sales growth and profitability. How to make sure that the effort of employers are appraised from time to time to find out how they contribute to the achievement of organizational goals, and also raising educational qualifications for recruitment, selection, promotion and placement of workers more effective.

I assume that effective human resource management and facility management strategy enables employees to contribute effectively and productivity to overall company direction and accomplishment of the organization's foals and objectives. If every human resource related tasks or functions , such as recruitment, selection, orientation, training, appraisal, motivation functions can achieve perfect aims in the shorten time efficiently, then the organization will have implement one effective human resource department.

EFFECTIVE FACILITY MANAGEMENT BENEFIT:

This effectice HR related functions will ensure its stable continuity and achievement to the organization. However, I believe personal element is the main factor to raise organization's effectiveness to compare other kinds of factors, e.g. good machine facilities , good working environment, good employee morale and organizational policy etc. factors. If the organization has good qualities of personnel element. Consequently, the organization should prioritize the development of the human element to maximize talents, skills and ability which will automatically reflects on the company's profit. So, it seems that company's profit raising up or falling down , it has relationship to good or bad personnel element. One firm seems to be an auto-mental machine factory, it needs to employ some people , through a conventional plant with similar capacity might require more people. So, the company (factory) needs good personnel element for proper HR planning to employ the suitable workers to do the right job positions, it is known as a "manpower planning".

Hence, training is one important function to some organizations, when the organization needs to train lacking technicians or raise to improve their modern skills of improve upon their talents and educational qualifications when it selects to employe these low skillful employees to do its any departments' high technical skillful jobs when the organization needs to change. Thus, the technical workers need to be equip themselves skills which will boost quality product and profit making of their organization.

If focuses on raising raising productivity through improved quality, efficiency , cost reduction, and enabling customers concentrate on their core business activities, such as one vehicle manufacture factory needs have one effective training deparment to train whose vehicle manufacturing workers to learn how to apply artificial intelligence (AI) technological robots to manufacture good quality vehicles number to supply to overseas markets to sell in short time efficiently. Thus, the vehicle factory focuses on raising vehicle number productivity through improved artificial intelligence and skillful workers' skills to achieve raising vehicle quality in efficient way, and reducing employee number and salary cost and satisfying vehicle customers' different kinds of new vehicle design driving needs from artificial intelligent technological manufacturing.

However, some business is full of uncertainty and understanding of labour contribution or human resources development to training / raising management level staffs' managerial skills of boosting organizational productivity and as well as its profitability . I believe raising managerical skills to managers, which will assist to whom to raise effective productivity or efficiency to different departments. Why can training raise or improve managerial skills to managers ? The reasons are that the challenges of lack of skilled labour, heavy competition among firms, technological problem, low productivity and then rate of poor performance and poor product implementation when placing a serious limitation on product expansion and increase increase in productivity. If the organizatin has no enough high managerial skillful level of managers to know why and how to manage their team members to work efficiently in the organizational structural high technological changing working environment. Then, the poor skillful employees won't adapt to work in high technological changing working environment, such as artificial intelligence manaufacturing working environment. Then, it will be reduce productivities inefficiently, due to lacking high level owning managerial skillful of managers to supervise or lead them to work in one high managerial efficient way.

Hence, future HR development to train or raise managerial skills to different department managers. it seems to need have one essential HR training policy to any organizations if they hope to innovate to rsise productivity and efficiency successfully. I assume that the effective human resource development can enhance productivity in order to avoid poor performance as well as efficiency of human resource training to managers can result in organizational growth.

An effective HRM involve maintaining and improving all aspects of a company's practices. Hence, HR manager must devise the most efficient and cost -effective means of hiring, e.g. advertising and recruit for vacant positions. HR management team must devise and implement the selection procedures to choose the mot suitable candidates establish paying welfare and salary policy efficiently.

What factors can influence employee performance appraisal system? Has it relationship between good employee performance appraisal system and raising productivity or improving efficiency? One effective employee performance appraisal system can let human resource department to raise service efficiency to assist the organization to raise whole human resource long term development (human planning). An effective performance appraisal system can meet targets to acceptable quality standards and benchmarks as determined in each category of human resource service delivery. One effective employee performance appraisal system should be supported by training of staff, particularly those with managerial and supervisory responsibility , and the process should be regarded as interactive for multural agreement between supervisors and appraisers.

In fact, if one organization has one effective employee performance appraisal system, it can encourage employees to work hard, raise efficiency and productive performance more easily. It is one good tool for human resource management and performance improvement. The process of performance management involves the identification of common goals between the appraiser and the appraisee. It must relate to the overall organizational goals. To test each employee performance, such as if a process is conducted effectively. It will increase productivity and quality of output when the department(S) staffs who had ever participated the process. Hence , the performance appraisals , accuracy and fairness in measuring employee performance is very important. Performance management is a control measure used to determine which work tasks with a view of taking corrective action. It is also used to reflect on past performance as the organization plans ahead. So, provision of feedback on the required corrective action to let every employee to know whether why and how he/she has done error in order to let he/she to revise whose error is critical in the process. For the appraisals to be effective, the top management must be supportive in providing information, clear performance standards must be set, the appraisals must not be used for any other purpose apart from performance management and the evaluation must be free from any rating biases. However, comparing the employees' performance from the performance appraisal is important in making future improvement. The performance appraisals are supported to be conducted at least twice annually to be better than once annually. The annual performance appraisals also need to help in determining how every employee fits into the organizational development and efficiency in performing all the assigned tasks and responsibilities. Moreover, it also needs to help in determining the training needs of the employees in planning future job schedules.

Additionally, the kind of working environment that is needed to be created by the performance appraisals optimizes the employees' work performance. Then, departmental and individual objectives are needed to formulate which will be consistent with the organizational objectives. In fact, training is one method to raise employee performance. The raters should be trained on various aspects, like supervision skills, conflict resolution, coaching, setting performance standards, linking this system to pay, and how to provide employee feedback. The training will equip ratees with expertise and knowledge what they need in making decision in the course of the process.

What factors will influence employee performance appraisal system successfully? They include formal meetings factor, individual performance should need be discussed. The performance review may include the actual performance, the tasks that are completed and areas that need improvement. It aims to achieve " action inquiry" to let employee individual or every team has chance to enquire whether how to improve productive performance questions in order to earn more effective recommendations. The another factor is feedback, it is an important part of one effective employee performance appraisal systems. The feedback should be specific and timely and be against the predetermined performance expectations. So, every employee has right to know how who are progressing in performing the assigned tasks and to receive feedback. However, feedback should need to be provided on a continuous basis, e.g. daily, weekly or monthly more better than two weekly or half year period.

In conclusion, poor performance evaluation won't havve the desired effect. There should be a proper development of the appraisal to remove subjectivity and bias in the ratings. Because the appraiser's subjective bias will cause the inaccurate measurement to every staff individual actual performance to decide whether he/she ought need to be promoted or not. Hence, removing subjectivity and bias in the ratings of appraiser personal poor performance evaluation factor will be very important to achieve one effective employee performance appraisal plan to bring either positive efficient method.

● Effective facility management on employee performance

An effective training and good training room environment can maximize the job performance. Every organization's respensibility to enhance the job performance of the employees and certainly implementation of training and development is one of the majoe steps that most companies need to achieve this organizations need to utilize human resourcee effectively. Traning of human resource needs to fit into the organization's structure as this it will make the organizations achieve their goals and objectives.

For telecommunication industry case example, how to carry on one effectively training into raise employee efficiency. It includes their questions: What training programs exist the telecommunications section? What are the training objectives? What methods are used and do these methods meet the training objectives? How does training affect employees performance? Why does telecommunication industry employees need better training? Training is a type of activity which is planned a systematic and it results in enhanced level of skill, knowledge, and competency that are necessary to performance work effectively.

In telecommunication organization, staffing needs to ensure that the right people are available at the right time in the right place. This involves identifying the nature of the job and implementing a recruitment and selection process to ensure a correct match within the organization. Training and development are often used to chose the gap between current performance and expected future performance. How does training and development provide performance feedback, identifying individua strengths/ weaknesses, recognizing individual performance, assisting in goal identification, evaluating goal achievement, identifying individual training needs, determining organizational training needs, improving communication and allowing employees to discuss concerns?

There are a number of alternative sources of appraisal includes: Training telecommunication front line staffs, supervisors, managers appraisal are done by an employee's manager one level higher, self appraisal performance done by the employee prior to the performance interview, subordinate appraisal: appraisal of a supervisor is by an employee, which is more appropriate for developmental than for administrative purposes. Peer appraisal is by follow employees for use in an interview conducted by the employee's manager, team appraisal based on total quality management concepts, recognizing team accomplishment's rather than individual performance, customer appraisal that seeks evaluation from both external and internal customers.

Training is a planned and systematic modification of behavior through learning events, activities and programs which result in the participants achieving the levels of knowledge, skills, competencies and abilities to carry out their work effectively. The main purpose of training is a acquire and improve knowledge, skills and attitudes towards work related tasks. It is one of the most important potential motivators which can lead to both short-term and long-term benefits for individuals and organizations. It can raise high morale, employees who receive training have increased confidence and motivations, lower cost of production, training eliminates risks because trained personnel are able to make better and economic use of material and equipment thereby reducing and avoiding waste, lower turnover, training brings a sense of secutiry as the workplace, reduces labour turnover and absenteeism is avoided.

Change management, training helps to manage change by increasing the understanding and involvement of employees in the change process and also provides the skills and abilities needed to adjust to new situations, providing recognition, enhanced, responsibility and the possibility of increased pay and promotion, helping to improve the availability and quality of staff.

An effective training needs to focus on workers' performance, improving certain: working practices, this focuses on improvement regardless of the performance problems and changing or renewing the organization situation, which may arise because of innovations or changes in strategy. When the organization feels training need, it needs to create , develop maintain and improve any systems relevant in contributing to the availability of people with required skills. Moreover, training programs should be designed to carter for the different needs.

Furthermore, HR , the training programme, content and the trainees' chosen depend on the objectives of the training programme. There are two different methods that organizations may choose from for training and developing skills of its employees. There are on-the-job training given to organizational employees then conducting their regular work at the same working venues and off-the -job training involves taking employees away from their usual work environments and therefore all concentration to the training. Examples of the on-job training include but are not limited to job rotations and transfer, coaching and/or mentoring.

On the other hand, off-the job training examples include conferences, role playing. Different organizations are motivated to take or different training methods for a number of reasons for example: depending on the organization's strategy, goals and resources available, depending on the needs identified at the time and the target groups to be trained which may include among others individual workers, groups, teams department or the whole organization.

Job rotation and transfers is as a way of developing employee skills within organization involves movements of employees from on official responsibility to another for example taking on higher rank position within the organization, and one branch of the organization to another. For transfers for example, it would involve movement of employees from one country to another. These rotations and transfers facilitate employees acquire knowledge of the different operations within the organization together with the differences existing in different countries, where the organization operates.

The knowledge is acquired by the selected employees for this method is beneficial to the organization as it may increase the competition advantage of the organization. In every training, trainees are provided with some information related the description of the roles, concerns objective, responsibilites, emotions.

In conclusion, effective training needs have these requirements, identifying and defining training needs, defining the learning required in terms if what skills and knowledge have to be learnt and what attitudes need to be changed, defining the objectives of the training, planning training programs to meet the needs and objectives combination for training technique and locations, deciding who provides the training, evaluating training amending and extending training as necessary.

● How facility management
assists organizations to
raise productive efficiency

In any organizations, instead of their human resource department function includes: interview, selecting, training, peformance evaluation management, reward management etc. based human related responsibilities. Can human resource department assist any other departments to raise employee individual productivies and efficiencies, the organization lacks one effective facility management department? Although, it has only indirect relationship to productivity and efficiency issue. It does not represent that it can not assist any departments to attempt to raise employee individual productivity and efficiency, if it lacks one facility management department. I shall indicate evidences to explain how it will possible occur.

How to impact human resource (HR)management on turnover productivity and corporate financial performance? I believe that HR development has an economically and statistically significant impact on both intermediate employee outcomes (turnover and productivity) and short and long term measures of corporate financial performance.

In fact, the impact of human resource management policies and practices on firm performance is an important topic in the fields of human resource management. The high performance work practices may include comprenhensive employee recruitment, selection procedures, incentive compensation and performance management system , and implementing employee engagement, training strategies, which can improve the knowledge, skills, and abilities of a firm's current and potential employees. However, when many employees work in one poor office or warehouse working environment in long time, then poor working environment will influence their performance to be poor.

However, arguments made in related research are that a firm's current and potential human resources are important considerations in the development and execution of the firm's strategic plan. It brings this question: How and why organization's human resource development plan which can assist to raise employee individual productive efficiency. I shall assume that one organizational human resource policies, if it is effective, then it can bring properly contribution to provide a diect and economically significant contribution to the firm.

An organization's effective HR department development and facility management strategy is needed to support by the development and vaidation of an instrument that reflects the system of high performance work practices adpted by the firm's employees. Then, if the organization has high performance work practices, it implies that its all employees had adopted its working environment to do every task efficiently. The reasons include as below points:

The first point, their employees must add value to the firm's production processes from effective training methods to achieve raising levels of individual performance successfully.

The second point, the skills to the firm seeks must be rare. So, the firm's employees can have rare skills to contribute to their organization to compare the other similar industry's organizations, their owning general ordinary skills of employees. So, rare skillful employees and effective training both methods which will be important factors to assist different departments to improve performance and raise productive efficiency more easily. Also, it implies that an effective Hr department will have above characteristics when the organization's human resource department owns above these competitive advantages. Then, achieving the raising productivity and efficiency aim will achieve more easily.

The third point, the human resource department and facility management department needs to have long-term human capital development to invest to the firm's employees to continue to train them to improve their hard and soft both skills. Investments in human resource development, they are similar to organization's equipment or facilities investments. So, they both are such as to invest in the firm's specific human captial, which can further decrease the probability of such imitation by qualitatively differentiating between the firm's specific talent employees and the other same industry firms' employees .Thus, it means that the firm's employees' skills and efforts will be better to compare its same industry competitors' employees, if the firm has long-term human resource talent development strategy to its different departments' employees to prepare to raise heir skills and efforts level.

The final point, a firm's human resources must not be subject to replacement by technological development, e.g. artificial intelligence, computer, information technology, internet or other substitutes of they are to provide a source of competitive advantage. Although, when the organization can choose to apply technologies investment to replace all employees or many employees to do their tasks in order to manufacture any products. However, the labor saving technological method is not suitable to half-service industry. For example, a restaurant can use robots to replace waitors to deliver food to clients to eat. It is simple food delivery tasks. But it is not good to apply robots to replace cookers to do their cooking tasks, because robot cooker's cooking skill, it is difficult to imitate human cooker's cooking skill in order to make same or similar ,even better food taste to let restaurant clients to feel better food taste. For the restaurant's cashier task example, because casher;s calculation ability will be netter to compare (AI) 's calculation ability. Human cashier's calculation error chance will be lesser to compare robot cashier's calculation skills. So , if the restaurant's all cookers, waiters and cashiers whose tasks all are replaced by robots. It will bring under utilized consequence because robots can not perform above their maximum potential more easier than human employees in the restaurant's long term working hours every day, because the restaurants employ more than one staff to prepare to replace the staff when he/she feels tired to need rest. Otherwise, these all restaurant positions , it has only one robot to do its position in the restaurant. I believe that these three cashier and cooker and waitor robots will be used to the maximum of utilization , then they will be older and calculation, walking and cooking speed and effort will also be slow and poor when they are used long hours every day to serve clients in the restaurant.

Thus, when one service organization, it can not only concentrate on robots to replace human employees to do their positions' all tasks. It will perform worse than the service organizaion , it only uses robots to replace some employees to do some tasks and some positions still use human employees to do themselves tasks. Otherwise, one manufacturing organization, e.g. car manufacturing organization, it may apply robots to participate some part of human employees' manufacturing tasks in the car manufacturing process. It will help human empoyees to manufacturing can productivities and efficiencies more than the another car manufacturing firm only employs human workers to manufacture all cars in car manufacturing process every day. When the later car manufacturing neglects to apply robots to participate the whole car manufacturing process to assist human workers to manufacture cars. Then, the later only applying human workers' car manufacturing firm which will have worse productivities and inefficiencies to compare the prior car manufacturing firm to apply both robots and human workers to manufacture any kinds of cars in whole car manufacturing process. The reason is because human workers must feel tried when they need concentrate their nevous to manufacture many cars every day. If robots can participate their car manufacturing tasks to share work load to assist they to finish some more difficult or complex part of tasks, then they will feel less nervous and they reduce pressure to manufacture the complex part of car manufacturing process. Then, their efficiency and productive performance will be raised in possible.

● Predictive analytics when the organization feels its human resources need to be changed.

The third point to raise efficiency and improve productive factor is that the organization feels need to know how it ought need to spend time and human resources to gather external environment and internal data to predict when the suddent environment changes to influence insufficient productivities and poor performance is caused from unpredictive poor environment change factor influence.

Jac, F.E & John, R.M. (2014, pp.13-16) explained that if any organizations expected they can adapt any external poor economic environment as well as organization's weakness causing changing factors to bring their organization's inefficiencies and poor productive performance causing in long term. They need to know and learn how to predict their HR needs when their HR is needed to be changed in order to adapt the sudden external economic environment changing and organization's weakness to cause its inefficiency and low productive performance consequence.

Any organization needs to gather datas concern: What will be needed to be lead potentially? What are the future market demands? What are the leader's changing managing attitude to let whole company's staffs to adapt easily in order to encourage they raise efficiency and improve productive performance more easily? It also needs to predict when the external forces drives will occue to cause how it's human resource strategy needs to be changed to adapt or fight the sudden external forces drives influence in order to avoid inefficiency or low productive performance consequence. The external force drives may include: Slow encourage growth, technological labour shortage, customer complaints number increasing, new competitors' products existing or enter the market, government regulation prohibition. Then, the organization gathers all these external environment forces drives datas to predict when these poor external environment changes will occur.

On the one hand, it can implement human resource changing strategy, such as reducing workforce, new skills needed, increasing training, focusing on service, informing employees new benfits regulations. On the other hand, it needs to change the internal drives factors, due to the external forces drives sudden change influence that it feels it needs to change its human resources strategy in order to avoid inefficiency or/and low productive performance causing. However, it also needs to find whether its organizational internal drives factors also need to be changed to avoid inefficiency and/or poor productive performance causing. The internal drivers factors may include: Whether the company itself needs to change new company vision, due to external environment changes, whether it needs to change its leadership gap to adapt sudden external environment factors influence, whether its organizational culture and brand image and finances sources and expenditure controlling need to be changed , due to external environment changes influence factor.

However, when the organization discovers that it needs to change its human resource strategy in order to adapt the sudden economic environment poor changing influence. Then, it needs to explain to let its employees to know whether why and how and what aspects, it needs to change, how to implement accelerate development to adapt the possible sudden economic environment poor changing occurrence, when it is the right time to begin transformation, reimplement to wage/salary payment policy and evaluation performance method, due to the possible sudden poor economic environment changing influence. Hence, when the organization can predict when the external poor economic environment changes influences to cause the inefficiency and poor productive performance consequence, then it can know how to change its human resource strategy in order to adapt the possibe sudden poor economy environment changing influence to cause inefficiency and poor productive performance causing consequence in possible.

● Good working place environment and no sex labor different treatment factor

One good working place environment is another important factor to influence employee individual performance and efficiency to be improved. I assume that selected the best skillful workers to do the tasks, but it is not represent these best skillful workers must raise efficiency to do their tasks .

Fiona, M.W, (2004, p.79) indicated one case to explain why skillful working won't be possible to raise efficiency to work , if the organization's workplace environment is poor and it implements unfair sex treatment to employ workers between male and female sex and different country. The case concerns one factory employed over 2,000 workers, women made up nearly two-thirds of these workers. Nearly, half the workers were other country, e.g. Asian. The division of labour was clear, when the Western country, e.g. US men were knitters, mechanics, dyers and top managers. The Asian women workers in the finishing process in personnel, and white collar jobs.

The finished jobs women did-were low paid, repetitive and based upon piece production, which is conceived of as a natural attribute, not a skill, they joined fabric together, bar-tasked herms, and operated button-sewing machines. An Asian woman might sew side seams all day, every day, for weeks at a time, unlikely the assembly line that controlled the flow of work, the machinist wzs dependant on the supervisor to bring work to her. This could be caused frustration to the factory's women labour. The individual worker had no control over what she would do not tried to boost her speed on each operation in order to secure the highest rate for the job. The women disliked bring moved between jobs , but management looked for flexibility in the use of their labour power.

However, the work environment was physically tiring, noisy and monotonous. This was a common response to the job . The Asian women were expected to meet targets of production each day and had to work under pressure to earn a bonus. Monotony was eased through conversation, jokes. The Asian women's work was domesticated by them. For example, the factory manager feels the female workers seem to be very machine and tells them you are my machine. So, it causes the factory Asian female workers feel angry and complain the Western , US manager's verbal joke behavior is poor to cause the Asian women workers have negative emotion to do ths factory job often.

Hence , it explains that why this factory Asian female workers won't raise efficiency in possible, due to its unfair job treatment, the factory management high level positions are selected to US male applicants to do. So, the Asian female workers will feel unfair position treatment and they feel they won't earn promotion chance, even they have effot to do any managment positions to replace these US male managers in this factory . Morevover, their factory managers' attitudes are poor to let them to feel often. The US managers often speak to them, such as my machine. They have not said high value Asian female workers to let them to feel they are important employees in this factory 's manufacturing deparment. Hence, their emotions will be influenced to be poor and spend less effort to hard to work to raise piece productivity in order to earn bonus , due to they feel tried to work , because they have no rest time in this factory. Finally, the poor working environment , it lacks good air condition facilities to let them to feel more cool feeling to comfort to work in summer or warm heater facilities to let them to feel warm feeling to comfort to work in winter. Moreover, machines' sound cause noise pollution to cause them to feel ear listening physical illness when they need to work in noisy workplace workplace in long term in possible.

All these poor psychological and physical both factors will influence the skillful Asian female workers to perform poorly. Hence, it seems this factory needs to change its employment strategy to let the Asian female workers have fair employment chance to apply the manager positions in this factory. It aims to let the Asian female workers feel they have promotion chance to promote to do any low, middle and high level of management positions and attempt to manage the Western male workers to do the hand-needed productive tasks.

This factory may arrange one training department. For example, the training department can provide factory manager's managing skillful training courses to teach the high potential Asian female workers to be promoted to do the management level positions. So, they have chance to be promoted to the high level management position from the middle level and low level management position in this factory. So, the fair position promotion , salary reward and improved factory's facilities, e.g. increasing factory spaces, increasing machine number, increasing warming heaters and air conditoners number these factory facility management issues will influence the Asian female worker individual efficiency and productive performance to be improved in possible.

However, this factory management will need to solve the most important influential poor performance or inefficiency workplace environment facilities problem in the factory, the organization must need to change in order to let these Asian female workers feel comfortable environment to work in this factory. The maintenance system to improve the factory's workplace environment to be felt more comfortable to these female workers. The type of tasks may include: Inspection for leaks in hydraulic system, predictive maintenance, scan all electrical connectons with infrared, cleaning and removing debris from machine, taking reading rcord of machine operating every day time, scheduled replacement and removing replace pump every three years, interviewing the operator to enquire how machine is operating, carrying on analysis concerns how a type of machine performance history analysis. So, these factory's facility management tasks are important factor to let these Asian female workers to feel safe to work in this factory,when this factory female workers feel this workplace environment is improved to be more safe and comfortable as well as their illnesses are reduced and promotion. Ths another review point is that many Western male manager individual behavior and attitude is changed to let them to feel better and the training course is effective to let them to feel skillful level is raised . Then, the skillful Asian female worker individual piece productive number will be raised as well as the low skillful Asian female worker individual productive performance will be improved, due to the organization has effective training courses to let them to learn how to raise their skills to produce every piece of product in efficient way.

● How can school's rooms facility provide comfortable rooms learning environment to raise educators' teaching efficiency?

These are considered questions concern school organiations : Must school's training deparment need to be arranged? How can school organizations' human resource department help educators determine cost (efficiency) , how to define student performance (effectiveness) and how to compare cost to raise high quality of teaching performance to teachers? Has it relationship how to guide policy and allcation of resources between school organizations' human resource strategy and the structure that produce the greatest improvement to teacher individual teaching behavior for the least cost to satisfy student's learning need?

I beleive that school's human resource deparment has relationship to influence teacher individual teaching performance and student's individual performance in eduation industry. The teaching effect to teacher's performance includes: high cost and high performance or high cost and low performance or low cost and high performance or low cost and low performance.

However, these unpredictive variable factors will bring above these teaching effect to be changed, even the school's human resource department had selected the teacher who owns more years teaching experience and high level of qualification to teach the subject. It means that the high level qualification and owning more teaching experience's teacher can teach whose students in poor teaching performance to bring poor learning effectiveness to whose students. The unpredictive variable factors may include socio-economic make up of student high populations, so the prior excellent performance teacher needs to teach 30 students in one classroom in prior. Currently, he/she needs to teach 50, even more tham 50 students number in one classroom, due to the shortage of teachers number and/or increasing students number to the school , size of school, e.g. classroom number is no increasing change, but the students number is increasing to the school, teacher turnover ratio increases, it is possible that many teachers feel pressure to teach many students in one classroom. They want to change career development, they feel unfair salary and benefit treatments, they are complained by students of student's family, they feel themselves teaching studetn's learning performance, it can't improve and examinatons results are worse. They teachers concrn themselves' teaching responsibilities more than students themselves learning responsibilities as well as the mobility of students, e.g. many students often change different subjects to learn or many students are leaving this school and they change to another new school to learn. So, the teacher needs to spend much time to teach the new students , due to they are replaced to the leaving old students as well as the teacher needs to spend much time to teach the new student swhen he/she is studying this new subject and he/she is the another old subject student. So, these unpredictive variable factors will cause the owning past excellent teaching performance's teachers feel pressure to teacher his/her students currently. If any one of above these unpredictable factors influence to his/her teaching behavioral needs to be changed to in order to adapt this sudden new and complex's teaching workplace or learning environment. Then, it is possible that their teaching performance will be worse, due to they feel pressure to teach their students in classroom every day.

So, it seems that it has no relationship between the effective human resource department's application selection process and the training course' content and the teacher's teaching performance because all of above these factors can not predicted when one of them will occur in order to find solutions to solve these problems in prior. Moreover, it also explain that teacher individual teaching performance has no direct relationship to human resource department, because one excellent teaching performance teacher will have possible to be influenced his/her teaching performance to be poor, due to any on of above these factors influence.

Reference

Bernard, M.B. & Bruce, J. A. (1994) Improving organizational effectiveness through transformational leadership: US. Sage publications, Inc. pp. 11-13.

Fiona, M.W. (2004). organizational behavior and work , a critical introduction, 2 ed. : New York, US, Oxford university press, pp.79 .

Jac, F.E.& John , R.M. (2014) predictive analytics for HRM:US Pearson Education pp.13-16

Stephen, P.R. & Timothy, A.J. (2018). Essentials of organizational behavior, 14 ed.: US. Pearson Education, Inc. pp.108-110.

CHAPTER TWO

FACILITY MANAGEMENT CAN REDUCE MAINTENANCE SERVICE EXPENDITURE

Facility management provides a variety of non core operations and maintenance services to support any organizations' operation. For logistic organization example, it is possible to provide effective maintenance service to warehouse in order to reduce warehouse facilities to be damaged to bring to spend to buy any new equipment facilities expenditure. So, when the logistic company's warehouse facilities can be maintenance to be the best quality. Then, they can be used these warehouses' machines facilities again. Their performance can assist workers to manufacture any products to keep the most efficiently an raising the best production performance in whole manufacturing process. Then, this logistic company's facility management department can bring to avoid purchase any new machine facilities expenditure spending. One to these warehouses' production machine facilities are kept in the best production performance environment even in long term production need.

The logistic industry's facility management department can create cost savings and efficiency of the warehouse's workplaces. It's machines facilities (production machines) are dealt with the maintenance management of the physical assets maintenance service. FM (facilities management) has been being applied to industrial facilities in logistic and warehouse industry long term as well as maintenance plays a significant role to ensure the full service and the warehousing system, including both building components and equipment in warehouse.

Maintenance service is needed to bring a certain level of availability and reliability of a warehouse facilities system and its components and its ability perform to a standard level of quality. So , it seems that logistic industry's warehouse asset cost reducing. It depends on whether it has one facility management department to provide maintenance service to itself warehouse workplace's production machine facilities and warehouse building itself in order to let workers t feel the manufacturing machines can bring good manufacturing performance to assist them to produce any products in one safe warehouse workplace environment. Hence, the performance measurement of warehouse maintenance issue will be valued to be consider to every warehouse manager and facility manager in logistic industry.

In logistic industry, (FM) works at two level on the one hand, it provides a safe and efficient working environment, which is essential to influence warehouse workers whether how they perform to do their manufacturing tasks or logistic goods delivery tasks in warehouse. When they feel the warehouse is safe environment to work. They will not need to consider anywhere has risk to cause they die by accident in warehouse. Hence, they can concentrate on doing their every tasks . On the other hand, it can involve strategic issues, such as property (warehouse workplace and management, strategy property decision and warehouse facility, e.g. manufacturing machine, facility maintenance and checking planning and maintenance planning development.

However, reducing the operating expense issue will be the main aim when the logistic company feels that it has need to set up one in-house facility management department to carry on any maintenance service for its warehouses' any workplace property and manufacturing machines facilities. So, when the logistic company decides to implement one facility management department, it needs to ensure its facility management department can bring the minimum level of keeping manufacturing performance and efficiency to its warehouses' any manufacturing machines and warehouses' property to avoid to be damaged in short term, such as loss of business due to failure in service, provision of project to customer satisfaction, provision of safe environment, effective utilisation of workplace space, e.g. warehouse effectiveness and communication between the workers and the logistic managers in the warehouse workplace , due to the warehouse's space is not enough maintenance service reliability to the logistic company's warehouse, responsiveness of the warehouse's worker individual negative emotion problem, due to he/she often feels need to work in one unsafe warehouse working environment. Hence, it seems that poor or unsafe warehouse working environment can influence workers feel negative emotion to work to bring low efficiency (inefficiency) or under productive performance in warehouse. It has relationship to influence they to bring psychological negative emotion feeling to work when the organization lacks one effective warehouse management repairing service to be provided to the warehouse's facilities and properties' maintenance needs in order to avoid ineffective measurement and misleading of performance.

Hence, the logistic company's facilities management department often needs to be reviewed whether its maintenance service level is passed to achieve the lowest repair (maintenance) service standard to its warehouse itself property and manufacturing machine or warehouse delivery tool facilities or warehouse lamps' light whether is enough to let workers to see anything clearly to avoid accident occurrence or see anything to work clearly or the warehouse space areas are enough to let they can have enough space to walk or communicate to their team supervisors or deliver any goods more easily in the short distance between the worker's sending goods location and the delivering goods destination in order to avoid because the lacking enough space to cause the accident occurrence , due to the space is not enough to let they deliver their goods to any locations in warehouse.

Hence, it seems logistic company's (FM) department can contribute to the organization's mission, such as avoiding warehouse accident occurrence, inefficiency, not enough and unavailability of the facility for future needs when the warehouse lacks enough space areas to bring poor performance of facility and dangerous warehouse itself property in warehouse, e.g. safe and reliable operations of material handling equipment and maintenance of warehouse facilities, grounds, security system, utilities, plumbing, heating , enough lighting system, air conditioning, warming heater, fire protection, security system alarm etc. facilities in warehouse.

Hence, it seems that if the logistic company expected to reduce to spend lot of excessive manufacturing machine purchase expenditure, lose of workers' life or bring workplace accidents , due to poor warehouse workplace environment, even bringing lawsuit compensation claim loss , due to the worker individual accident or death is caused from the poor warehouse facilities, or bring negative emotion to let the workers feel they are working in unsafe warehouse workplace environment. Then, it ought choose to set up on facility management department in order to provide enough maintenance service to its warehouse to avoid these non essential expenditure causing , due to these poor warehouse facilities factors.

Hence any logistic company ought choose to set up one itself in

-house facility management department, it be better than outsourcing its all facilities service to one facility management (maintenance service provider) to help it to deal any kinds of maintenance service in warehouse. Because it is long term maintenance need to its warehouse's any machines and warehouse itself properties. If it chose to find one outsourcing facilitiy management maintenance service provider to replace its in-house facility management department to deal all related facilities maintenance tasks in warehouse. Then, it is possible that it needs to pay long time facilities maintenance service fee to its outsourcing facility management maintenance service provider more than itself facility management maintenance service provision department.

In conclusion, to decide whether the company ought need or not need facilities maintenance service or either set up in-house facility management department or outsource one facility management maintenance service provider. It depends on whether its organization has how many facilities are used in its workplace, how many staffs are working the workplace, how much size of its workplace, its workplace is office or warehouse or factory, how long time of its facilities' useful time etc. factors , then it can decide whether it needs or does not need one facility maintenance service department or outsourcing facility maintenance service provider to help it to deal any facilities management problem in its organization.

● Facility management role in
organization

When one company feels that it has need facility management service. It can choose to set up either in-house facility management department or seek one outsourcing facility management service provider to help it to arrange any facility management service need. However, this facility management role is only one for the organization. It concerns this question: What facility management maintenance function can bring the benefits to the organization?

It can define that all services required for the management of building and real estate to maintain and increase their value, the means of providing maintenance support, project management and user management during the building life cycle, the integration of multi-disciplinary activities within the built environment and the management of their impact upon people and the workplace. In traditional, (FM) services may include building fabric maintenance, decoration and refurbishment, plant, plumbing and drainage maintenance, air conditioning maintenance, lift and escalator maintenance , fire safety alarm and fire fighting system maintenance, minor project management. All these are hard services. Otherwise, cleaning , security, handyman services, waste disposal, recycling, pes control, grounds maintenance, internal plants. All these are soft services. Additional services, might also include: pace planning, things moving management, business risk assessment, business continuity planning, benchmarking, space management, facilities contract outsourcing service arrangement, information systems, telephony, travel booking facility utility management, meeting room arrangement services, catering services, vehicle fleet management, printing service, postal services, archiving , concierge services, reception services, health and safety advice, environmental management.

All of these services will be every organization's in-house facility soft or hard services needs. So, it explains why some large organizations feel need one effective facility management department to help them to arrange how to implement facility services efficiently in order to achieve cost reducing, raising efficiency and performance improvement aims because one effective facility management control system can influence employee individual productive effort to be raised or reduced indirectly.

However, (FM) can be selected either setting up one in-house (FM) department or outsourcing its services to one facility management service provider to help the organization to solve any kinds of facilities maintain service problems. One on-house (FM) department is a team, it needs employees to deliver all (FM) services. Some specialist services are needed to be outsourced, when the service is on expertise in the company. The no expertise services will be outsourced to simple service contracts, e.g. lift and escalator (FM) department will have direct labour, but it can outsource some specialist to help it to do some complex facilities management service. So, the team leader can of can manage whose team staffs, such as maintenance technicians run low risk operations . Otherwise, the outsourcing facility management service provider needs to help it to operate high risk operations or maintenance vital plant facility management service. Anyway, it can set up in-house (FM) department to arrange specialist direct labour and outsourced (FM) services to more than one facility management service providers to do different kinds of (FM) services. One of these outsourcing (FM) service provider, who can arrange sub-contractors to assist it to finish any (FM) services of it's outsourcing (FM) services are more complex to compare the other sub-contractors (third parties).

● What is a facility manager's role to provide quality service to satisfy its user needs?

We need to know how quality can be defined in facility management and why it should be defined by the customer? How facility managers can find out customer (user) needs? What are the difficulties in finding out users' needs and in delivering quality services? Whether improving quality always means requiring higher cost?

In general, facility manager's major responsibilities may include these major functional areas: longer range and annual facility planning, facility financial forecasting, real estate acquisition and/or disposal, work specification, installation and space management, architectural and engineering planning and design, new construction and/or renovation, maintenance and operations management, maintenance and operation management, telecommunications integration, security and general administrative services. When the facility manager had implemented any one of these FM services for those user. How does he/she provide excellent (FM) service quality ot let whose users to feel satisfactory?

In fact, quality issues can not be considered without customer-oriented perspective service quality involves a comparison of expectation with performance. (FM) service quality is a measure of how well to service level delivered matches customer expectation. So, these issues are (FM) service user's general measurement level requirement. The (FM) manager needs to achieve these the minimum performance measurement level to satisfy whose (FM) user's needs.

However, (FM) service quality has three characteristics: Intangibility, heterogeneity, inseparability. But in fact, (FM) service delivered may be through tangible physical aspects, e.g. factory plant workplace building, machine equipment maintenance, intangible (FM) services, e.g. managing space moving in plant to let staffs to work, managing outsourcing cleaners to clean factory equipment. However, all (FM) service performance often varies, due to the behavior of service personnel. Hence, a well developed job specification and training can help to improve the consistence of services of (FM). Any (FM) production and consumption of many services may are inseparable and they are usually interactions between the (FM) client and the contact person from the service provider.

Hence, it seems that service quality is considered as hard to evaluate. In (FM) service quality, it includes physical quality and interactive non-physical service quality. Physical quality is tangibles: The appearance of the physical facilities, equipment, personnel and communication materials. Non-physical services quality means reliability: The ability to perform the promised service dependably and accurately; responsiveness means the willingness to help customers and provide promopt service to let user to feel; assurance mans the competence of the system in its credibility in providing a courteous and secure service and empathy means the approachability, ease of access and effort taken to understand customers' needs.

Hence, a good performance of (FM) manager , he/she ought satisfy the user's tangible and non-tangible both service quality needs. I recommend that he/she can attempt to predict what are the (FM) customer expects in each (FM) service needs. Then, it can make decision what aspect(s) will be the (FM) users major (FM) service need and what aspect(S) won't be the (FM) users major (FM) service need. Then, he/she can make more accurate decision to arrange time, human resource , cost spending amount arrangement whether when it ought concentrate on finishing the (FM) major service tasks as well as whether how he/she ought finish the major (FM) service tasks to be more easily, e.g. how to arrange staffs number to finish, how many the minimum staffs number is needed to be arrange the major (FM) service tasks, time arrangement is important factor, because it can influence whether he/she ought finish the major (FM) service tasks today or tomorrow or later in order to have enough time to finish other non-major (FM) service tasks. Instead of time management, staff number arrangement is also important factor , if he/she arranged the excessive staffs number to do the (FM) major services tasks, then it is possible that it will have shortage of staffs number to finish the non-major (FM) service tasks on the day. So, avoiding either major or non-major (FM) services can not finish on the day. The (FM) manager needs to predict when the major (FM) services and the non-major (FM) services which are necessary to be finished in order to have enough time and staffs to assist him/her to finish every day major and non-major (FM) service effectively. Then, the achievement of his/ her (FM) major and non-major tangible and non-tangible services , it will have more chance to be performed efficiently by his/her managed staffs.

In conclusion, in any organizations , (FM) manager needs have good predictable effort to evaluate whether when his/her managed team need to finish the major and/or non-major (FM) tasks as well as whether how he/she ought arrange the accurate time and staff number to finish any major and/or non-major (FM) service tasks on the day. Then, his/her leading of (FM) service team can be managed to work more efficiently in order to satisfy her/his (FM) service user's needs.

● How (FM) space moving management
can bring valued add to organizations

There are interesting questions: How (FM) can bring value-add to avoid loss or earn more profit to the organization? Can it influence employees to raise performance and improve efficiency ? Some organizations' (FM) service need which is necessary in order to let employees can raise productivity.

It is based on these assumptions: I assume the organizations have completely either outsourced or in-house their (FM) facility management departments will gain more effect on added value than they have no (FM) function as well as organizations have a strong coordination with the (FM) department will gain more added value than organizations with a weak coordination. Organizations in the profit aim can gain more added value than organizations in the not for profit aim sectors.

In fact, any organization is difficult to confirm it has relationship between improving performance, raising efficiency and owning (FM) function in its organization. (FM) could have to do with the attraction of easy but incomplete indicators of efficiency rather than the necessarily and less direct measures if the effectiveness and the relevance of space moving useful management, e.g. whether building has the enough space to let employees to move to work easy in order to raise efficiency, whether the building has excessive furniture and equipment number and they are putted on wrong places to be caused employees move difficulty in the building in order to influence productive performance.

However, how to arrange space moving management to equipment, e.g. copying machines, faxes, productive machines, they are putted on the locations where have enough space to let employees to move to another locations. For example, the building floor has more than 50 employees, but its space is not enough to let these 50 employees to move to any locations to let them to feel easily often. Then, it is possible to cause they feel nervous pressure and they can feel difficult to work , when they are working in a small office space or factory space or warehouse space. Then, the consequence will be under-predictive efficiency or poor performance to any one of these 50 employees in this office or factory or warehouse.

" Facility management is responsible for coordinating all efforts related to planning, designing, and managing buildings and their systems, equipment, and furniture to enhance. The organizations abilty to compete successfully in a rapidly changing world." (F.Becker)

The author explains equipment, workplace internal space designing, furniture space putting location arrangement will have possible to influence employee individual productive performance or efficiency to be raised or reduced in the workplace. Hence, it seems that, in the value chain (FM) belongs to the activity part of the firm. To make the facilities cooperation with each office or factory or warehouse using space moving facility management. Facility space moving management must be linked strategically, tactically and operationally to other support activity to add value to the organization's office or factory or warehouse space moving management arrangement more effectively.

Thus, how to arrangement space moving management issue it will have possible to influence the organization's employee individual productive performance and efficiency in whose workplace. It seems that (FM) space moving management arrangement have indirect relationship to influence the organization's employee individual performance and efficiency , due to they need often to work in the workplace, if they feel moving difficulty , or excessive equipment , furniture number is putting into the small office, factory or warehouse locations, or they feel the office or factory or warehouse has excessive (a lot of) staffs number to work in the small space of office or factory or warehouse. Then, they can not concentrate nervous on finishing every tasks in possible. In long term, their efficiencies will be poor or inefficiencies or their performance won't be improved or causing poor performance in possible.

Instead of the not enough space moving and excessive staffs number factor, it will bring another question: Can enough information systems equipment cause a more efficient and improved performance to the organization staffs in the workplace? I assume that the office has 100 employees and it has only ten copying machines. So it means that ten employees use one copying machine. Hence, it brings this question: Is it enough to provide only ten copying machines to average ten employees to use? It depends on other factors, e.g. whether any one of these 100 employees needs to print how many documents per day , whether the five copying machines' locations are far away to separate different locations or they are stored in one printing room in the office, whether the day has how many staffs are absent, whether the day has how many printing machine(s) is/ are broken to need to be repaired. Hence, these unpredictable external environment factors will influence whether the five copying machines number is enough to let these 100 employees to use in the office every day. Hence, facility manager ought need to spend to observe average their copying behaviors every day in order to make data record. Many employees need to use copy machines to print documents, average how many document's page number, they need to print, how much average time spending to print their documents, average how many staff absent number on the day. Even, if the all five copying machines are stored in the printing room, calculating the staffs number whether how many staffs need more than five minutes to walk to the printing room to print their documents many staffs need to spend five minute to walk to the printing room, and they have other urgent tasks to wait to finish. It is possible to influence their efficiency, due to they often need to spend more than five minutes to walk to the printing room to print documents. If there are many staffs need to often to print documents, but their printing task will have many time, e.g. 20 separate printing tasks. Then, they need to spend at least (20x5) 100 minutes to spend time to walk to the printing room to print their documents. It must influence that they should not finish the other urgent tasks on the day. If there are many staffs to spend much time to walk to the printing room in the least 20 separate printing time or more on that day. All the facility manager needs to evaluate whether all the five copy machines are stored in the printing room whether it is the best location decision or they ought need be separated to put on different office locations in their workplaces, even he/she ought need to evaluate whether it is enough copying machines number, when the office has only 5 copying machines. He/she ought need to buy more copying machines number to satisfy any one of these 100 employee individual copying task need.

In conclusion, effective office or factory or warehouse space moving facility management will be one part task of (FM) function. If the office or factory or warehouse can have accurate equipment, machine , furniture number to avoid excessive or shortage number problem to cause employees often feel moving difficult problem in their workplace when they need to move to another location to work in office or warehouse or factory as well as whether the staff needs often spend time to wait the another employee to use the copying machine to print whose document or fax machine to deliver whose document. Then, it is not that fax or printing machines number is not enough to provide the employees to use in the office or warehouse or factory workplace.

Hence, (FM) includes space moving facility management to equipment , machines, furniture number as well as choosing anywhere is(are) the suitable location (s) arrangement to putting or storing these facilities in workplace as well as decision of the staff number and the workplace area size whether it has excessive staffs number to cause these staffs need to work in the small area size of office or warehouse or factory workplace. So, the organization ought need to decide whether it needs to reduce the office's staffs number to let them to work in another more suitable locations in another workplace. Hence, all these facilities space moving management and staffs and workplace size issues will be (FM) manager's consideration issues, because these external environment factors will influence employee individual efficiency and performance to be poor to cause low valued to its organization in long term in possible .

Reference

Becker, F. (1990). " Facility management : a cutting edge field?" property management 8 (2): 25-28.

● Predictive the choosing right

data asset and (FM) analytics

solutions to boost public

transportation service quality

Can gather the choosing right data public transportation service station facilities asset and analytics, it can give recommendation to help any organization to boost service quality? (FM) analytics data can be applied to public transportation service industry to be supported how and why the train, train, ferry , ship, air plane, underground train public transportation tools' time arrival and leaving information notice board and automated ticket paying machines facilities are putting on or stored any where locations in order to boost passengers to feel their facilities locations are convenient to let them to buy tickets and see the arrival and leaving time for the next public transportation tool from the information notice electronic board machine. So, it seems that these public transportation tools' station facilities locations can influence passengers to feel the public transportation service company how to consider to its passenger's buying ticket needs and next public transportation tool's arrival and leaving time information needs in order to boost its passengers use service quality and let them to feel better service reliable performance in any train, tram, ferry , ship, underground tram, airplane stations.

As these public transportation service organizations need to learn data analytics represent an opportunity for its ticket paying machine equipment facilities as well as the next transportation tool arrival and leaving time information notice board electronic equipment facilities anywhere the locations are the most suitable to put on or store these equipment to let passengers to walk to the ticket paying machines to buy the ticket to catch the train, tram, underground train, ferry, airplane, taxi, ship more easily. So, they do not need to spend more time to find these facilities locations and spend more time to queue to wait to buy ticket to catch the public transportation tool in stations conveniently. Instead of where is the seeking ticket paying machine location, where is the next public transportation tool arrival and leaving information notice time , these both issues will be any public transportation tool's passenger's main needs.

Hence, how to spend time to seek where the next public transportation tool's arrival and leaving time information electronic notice machine location and where the ticket paying machine location , these both factors will influence any passengers' positive or negative emotion causing. For example, if the passenger feels difficult to find the ticket paying machine in the large area size train station or /and he/she feels difficult to find the train time arrival and leaving information to let him/her to know when the next train will arrive the station. Due to he/she feels difficult to find the train ticket paying machine, he/she needs to spend much time to find any one ticket paying machine in the train station. Then, it will influence him/her to choose another public transportation tool to replace the train public transportation tool, e.g. he/she can choose to catch tram, underground train, taxi, bus, ferry, taxi, ship to replace train. So, it seems ticket paying machine and time arrival and leaving information notice electronic equipment 's location putting or stored choice will be one factor to influence the passenger to choose another kind of public transportation tool to replace train at the moment. When, he/she feels that he/she arrives the destination in the most short time. Then, the public transportation service organization (FM) manager has responsibility to evaluate whether there are enough ticket paying machines number to let passengers do not need to spend more time to queue to buy tickets to catch the public transportation tool in short time as well as there are enough time arrival and leaving for next transportation tool to let passengers to know. It will be their concerning issues when they arrive the public transportation service tool's station.

Hence, predictive passenger individual walking behavior can help the public transportation service organization to choose whether where are the most convenient and attractive locations to let the ticket paying machines and the arrival and leaving time information electronic board machines to be putted on or stored in the suitable station positions in order to let many passengers can find these essential facilities in stations very easily. So, gathering data concerns passenger walking behavior in the public transportation service any stations, which can help the facility manager to make more accurate evaluation to attempt to predict whether where the locations are common places to let passengers to choose to walk daily or where the locations are not common places to let passenger to choose not to walk daily in general. Then, he/she can apply these data of different locations in the stations to evaluate whether anywhere they will have many passengers to choose to walk or whether anywhere they won't have many passengers to choose to walk in order to make more accurate decision whether anywhere are the most suitable locations to let the ticket paying machines and the time arrival and leaving information electronic board equipment to be putter on or stored in order to let them to feel it is so easier to let them to find.

Anyway, calculating each station's passenger number per day issue is important to predict whether where , there are many passengers choose to walk or where, there are not many passengers choose to walk in these different public transportation service stations in order to evaluate whether where the stations' different ought put on paying ticket machines or time arrival and leaving information electronic boards in order to let they feel very easy to buy tickets and seeing the next arrival and leaving time information for the kind of public transportation service tool conveniently in the different stations. Moreover, if the station has no enough ticket paying machines number to be supplied to let passengers need to spend more than ten minute time to wait to buy ticket to catch the kind of public transportation service tool in every queue every day. Then it will cause them to choose another kind of public transportation tool to catch go to working place or entertainment place to replace it to on that day. Then, it will cause these passengers who often do not like to queue in the kind of public transportation service tool's any stations, who will not choose to go to anywhere of this kind of public transportation service tool's any stations again. Hence, in long term this kind of public transportation service tool will lose many passengers. Thus, calculating each station's busy time of passengers number , which can predict when it is the busy time and it can make more accurate decision whether the station has need to increase enough ticket paying machines number in order to bring enough supply number to satisfy passengers' ticket purchase need in the busy time.

In conclusion, gathering above all stations' public transportation service equipment facilities number, storing positions data and every station's passenger walking behavior data, they are necessary to any public transportation tool service industry, because these equipment number and storing locations will influence them to make decisions to choose another kind of public transportation tool to replace it's transportation service if they often feel difficult to find these facilities in its different stations. Thus, it is part of task to facility manager's responsibility if the public transportation service organization expects it won't lose many passengers , due to these external environment factor influence and it also implies cheap ticket price does not guarantee the passengers will choose to catch this kind of public transportation service tool to go to anywhere.

The relationship between facility management and productive efficiency

It is one interesting question: Can facility management function bring benefits to raise productive efficiency to organizations? I shall indicate some cases to attempt to explain this possible occurrence chance as below:

● Facility management benefit to office workplace

In private organizations, when the firm has facility management department, whether it can bring efficient administration to influence clerks to work efficiently in office, e.g. reducing administrative time or shorten time to work in administrative processes, in order to achieve minimizing clerk number labor cost. How to design office facilities to let office staffs to feel comfortable to work and reducing their pressure to work. It seems that office working environment will influence office staff individual performance. If the office working environment could improve efficiency and creativity of services to satisfy office workers' comfortable working environment needs. It will reduce every administration manager's working pressure when he/she needs often to find methods to attempt to encourage whose administrative clerks to avoid to waste working time to do some non-major administration tasks.

Hence, how to design or allocate or arrange office any facilities' stored locations or whether how many equipment number is the enough to store in the locations, which will influence office employees' working attitude in order to raise or reduce their administration tasks efficiency indirectly, e.g. the office is clean or dirty, whether office reception has enough information telephone switchboard operation facilities, whether every clerk's table has enough computers number to supply to every to use, whether internet speed is fast or slow in order to let any employees can send and receive email to communicate or download any document from internet in short time, whether data processing and computer system maintenance service supply is enough to be repaired to employees' computers immediately when their computers are broken to wait repair, whether website editing facilities operation whether is enough to link to office every staffs in order to let any office staffs can apply internet to do their tasks conveniently in short time.

Hence, all of these general office equipment facilities whether they are enough supplied and their stored positions anywhere are the suitable to assist any clerks to work conveniently, they will influence every office employee's administrative and productive efficiency indirectly as well as all faxes, copying machines, computers, whether internet linking maintenance service time is short or long to prepare to any office employees to use conveniently any time, these different issues will also influence every employee individual efficiency in office. Hence, it concludes that office working environment, facilities supply number, facilities maintenance service and facilities location storing both factors will influence employee individual administrative productive efficiency in office.

● facility management benefits to service working environment

Can effective facility management improve service working environment to raise employee individual work performance? It is a concern about the quality of service to its customer question. The term" standards and goals" are often used to measure staff individual service performance whether he/she can serve to customers to let them to feel this staff's service performance or attitude is good or bad.

Is the service workplace working environment facilities enough, it will influence customer service staff individual performance.

For shopping center service industry case example, for this situtation, e.g. shopping center's facilities are enough or are placed to the suitable locations in order to let the shopping center's customers to feel comfortable to shopping when they enter this shopping center as well as whether the shopping center's facilities can influence the customer service staffs to serve whose shopping customers easily or difficult, due to whether the shopping center's facilities whether are adequate supplied or their locations are the best suitable positions to influence their service performance to let them to feel easier or comfortable to serve their customers in any large size shopping centers. For example, whether the lamps' lighting energy is enough to let the shoppers to feel safe to walk to visit any shops when there are many shoppers were walking to cause crowd and they feel difficult to walk to avoid any body contact to any one in busy time when the shopping center has no enough lights to let them to see anywhere in the shopping center's dark environment. Then it will influence customer service staffs to feel difficult to find any shopping center customers, e.g. when two shopping center customers are fighting in one location where is far away to the shopping customer service staffs and securities in the shopping center, because the shopping center is large and it has no enough light to let the customer service staffs and securities to find their frighting location to deal their fighting behavior and other shopping center's shoppers will feel very dangerous to walk their fighting location to avoid to close them. Then, it will has possible to cause death or hurt to any one of these two fighting shoppers ,even other shoppers' life. Because the shopping center's securities and customer service staffs who need to spend much time to find their fighting location, it will delay they can bring the policemen to their fighting location when they arrive this shopping center's destination in short time in order to solve their fighting behavior to influence all shoppers' life in this shopping center. Hence, the shopping center whether it has enough lamps number and the lamps' light whether is enough, these lighting facilities will influence any shopping center customer service staffs and securities who can spend less time to arrive any locations to deal any urgent matters.

For another situation in shopping center, if the shopping center has no enough paying telephone service facilities to supply shoppers to phone to anyone when they feel need to phone to any in the shopping center. Then, it will lead to some shoppers decide to find where the shopping center's reception's telephone to supply to them to phone call to anyone. If they are ten shoppers are waiting to use the shopping center's reception telephone to phone call to their friend or family within one minute. Thus, it will influence the reception customer service staffs feel difficult to arrange how to distribute the only one telephone to these ten shoppers to use to phone call their friend or family when they are queuing within their one minute waiting time in the shopping center's reception. If these ten shoppers can not use the reception telephone to phone call anyone. hen, they will feel dissatisfactory and complain to the reception service staffs politely. So, lacking enough facilities in the shopping center's any where, it will possible to influence their shopping centers' shoppers to feel all shopping center's service staff individual performance to be poor. It means that if the shopping center expects to improve customer satisfaction to its customer service staff's behavioral performance, it meets have enough facilities to be supplied in the shopping center to let its shoppers to feel it is one comfortable and safe shopping center. In conclusion, shopping center's facilities will have possible to influence shoppers' feeling to evaluate its customer service staffs to evaluate whether their service attitudes are good or poor indirectly.

● Can facility management improve productivity

The productivity means resources (input) is therefore the amount of products or services (output), which is produced by them. Hence, higher (improved) productivity means that more is produced with the same expectation of resource, i.e. at the same cost is terms of land materials, machine, time or labor. Alternatively, it means same amount is produced at less labor cost in term of land, material, machine, time for labor that is utilized. So, it brings this question: How can facility management improve productivity? I shall explain as these several aspects, it is possible to be improved productivity from (FM) successfully.

Improved productivity of farm land: If the farming land has better facility management to bring advantages by using better seed, better facilities of cultivation and most fertilizer. It is in the agricultural sense is increased (improved). So, facility management can bring benefits to any land resource to raise productivity in possible. It implies that the productivity of land used for better facility management of industrial purposes is said to have been increased if the output of products or service within that area of industrial land is increased output aim.

Improved productivity of material: If the factory has improved better equipment by facility management method to assist skillful workers to raise the manufacture cloth number, then the productivity of the cloth number is improved by (FM) method.

Improved productivity of labour: When the factory has good manufacturing equipment facilities to be supplied to improve methods of work to product more producing number per hour, then (FM) improved productivity of worker. Hence, in any workplaces, when organization has good facilities, it will influence employees to raise productivities in possible, because they need often to improved equipment facilities manufacture products to achieve higher production number aim.

● Can facility management raise bank employee
productivity

Bank workplace environment is busy, the bank counter service staffs need to contact many bank clients to help them to serve or withdraw money from bank's counters. Whether does the quality of environment in bank workplace will influence the determination level of employee's motivation, subsequent performance productivity in bank working environment. For example, if the bank's staffs need work under inconvenient conditions , it will bring low performance and face occupational health diseases causing high absenteeism and turnover.

In general, bank size is usually small, it will have many bank clients enter bank to contact counter staffs to need them to help them to save or withdraw money. So, it will bring air pollution the crowd queue in every bank counter challenge when the bank has many people are queue waiting in counters to queue. So, bank working condition problem relates to environmental and physical factors which will influence every bank counter staff individual working performance to serve bank clients satisfactory. However, bank staffs need to deal many documents concern every client personal data every day. So, they need to spend much time to use computer and painting machines. This is particularly true for these employees who spend most of the day operating a computer terminal in bank workplace. As more and more computers are being installed in workplaces, an increasing number of business has been adopting designs for bank offices installment. So, bank needs have effective facilities management design because of demand of bank staffs for more human comfort.

An good equipment facility management for bank staffs to use conveniently, it is assumed that better workplace environment can motives bank employees and produces better productivity. Hence, bank office environment can be described in terms of physical and behavioral components to influence bank staffs to work inefficiently. To achieve high level of bank employee productivity, bank organizations must ensure that the physical environment in conductive to bank different department organizational needs, facilitating interaction and privacy, formality and informality, functional and disciplinarily, e.g. house loan or private loan departments, counter service department, visa card application department.

Thus, in a high safe privacy facility management working environment will let different department bank staffs feel safe to worry about privacy loss in possible. So, the improving bank facility to bring safe and high privacy to avoid bank client individual loss in working environment issue, the facility management can be results to bring these benefits, such as in a reduction in a number of complaints and absenteeism and an increase in productivity.

● Can (FM) create value to organization?

(FM) can reduce managing facilities as a strategic resource to add value to the organization and its overall performance, e.g. saving the energy in building and take care of shuttle buses and parking facilities space management for , on economic efficiency and effectiveness, or good price and value for the organization.

If the organization expects to apply (FM) process to save energy, it depends on possible input factors, i.e. interventions in the accommodation facilities services. So, it seems that the organization expects to save its energy consumption in its building. It needs have good space management facilities between parking its shuttle buses in its property's car park.

Why does space facility management is important to influence efficiency and productivity. For one school's building example, when the school decides none of the two gymnasiums student sport entertainment centers to be built in order to reduce financial cost and higher benefits. Remarkably, the use of space with the school overall strategic goals , such as creating spaces that better can support the teaching, motivate students and teachers, attract more students and increase the utilisation of existing space to accommodate an increasing number of students.

If it hopes to make high quality teaching facilities on student's choice where to study. The school will need to choose to build either one comfortable and new design facility teaching accommodation or build two gymnasium sport entertainment centers in its limited land space either for students' learning or sport aim. Due to it feels new teaching accommodation can make more attractive to increase students numbers to choose it to study more than building two new gym sport centers to let them do sport in school.

Hence, space choice (FC) management strategy will be one important considerable issue, when the organization has limited land space resources to make choose to build any constructions in order to increase many clients number. Such as the school organization has limited storage land resource to let it to build either two gymnasium sport entertainment centers or one new teaching accommodation in order to attract many students to choose it to learn. Hence, it needs to gather data to make more accurate evaluation to decide how to apply its space facility to choose to build these both kinds of buildings in order to achieve the attractive student learning choice aim, so whether the two sport entertainment activity centers or one new teaching accommodation choice, it needs to gather information to decide whether the school ought to choose to build which kind of building in order to achieve the increase of student number aim, so space facility management will be this school's land shortage problem.

CHAPTER THREE

THE RELATIONSHIP BETWEEN FACILITY MANAGEMENT AND CONSUMER BEHAVIOR

How and why shop facility management can influence consumer individual shopping behavior? If it is possible, what shop facility management factors can influence their consumption decision when they enter the shop to plan to buy anything. I shall indicate some shop case studied to explain whether how and why every shop's facility management can influence consumer individual consumption desire when any one consumer enters any shops.

● Shop's low ceiling height location (FM) influence consumer behavior

Can the shop's ceiling height influence shoppers' shopping behavior? Can the shop's variation in ceiling height can influence how consumers process information to decide to make purchase decision in the shops, e.g. for this situation, when the consumer enters the shop, he/she feels the ceiling height is low and it has a lamp will contact his/her head in possible. So, he/she chooses to move far away from the low ceiling location in the shop. It is possible that shop's ceiling low height and the lamp locates at the ceiling low height position will influence many customers' choices to leave the low ceiling height and lamp location, then the shop's low ceiling height will have possible to influenced many customers to choose to find the another shop to buy the similar kind of products , due to the lamp locates in the low ceiling height, so this lamp and low ceiling height will be possible factor to influence any shoppers who won't choose to walk to this dangerous location in the shop. If the shop's all spaces are ceiling height and it has many lamps are located at the low ceiling height spaces. Then, it will be serious to cause many shoppers do not want to spend too much time to choose any products in the shop because they feel dangerous to walk to the any low ceiling height lamps' locations in the shop.

Hence, hoe to design the different concept may be activated by the showroom ceiling if it were relatively high, as it tends to be in mall stores, versus low, as it is in most strip mall shops and outlet centers. Relatively high ceilings may bring safe shopping emotion to let any consumers to feel thoughts related to freedom, whereas lower ceilings may let consumers to feel dangerous to walk the locations in any shops. Hence it seems any shops ought not neglect whether their ceiling height is tall and the lamps ought avoid to locate in any low ceiling height locations in order to influence consumers number to be decreased.

● Can house facility management influence consumer individual purchase intention?

When one new property is built, whether the property consumers will consider how the new property is facility to influence their purchase intention to the property will the new property's (FM) influence buyers in real estate markets' preferences choice and living interest. Any new property's internal characteristics of the house unit itself , such as rooms available, when example, of external are location, accessibility to utilities services and facilities will have possible to influence the property buyer's final property purchase decision, so it seems that even the property price is cheap, it is not represent the property buyer will choose to buy the property, if he/she feels the property's facility management is poorer to compare other similar kinds of properties.

So, it can help real estate analysts better explain and predict the behavior of decision makers in real estate markets. Property consumers will search for property information, concerns the property's quality, price distinctiveness, ability, facility management, service of the property's external environment to decide whether the property is high value to choose to buy to compare other kinds of properties.

However, the external environmental forces, such as limited resources, e.g. time or financial will influence whose property consumption choice and living the property's satisfaction feeling (represent) a feedback from post-property purchase reflection used to inform subsequent decisions. The process of the property buyer's leaving experience will serve to influence the extent to which the property consumer how to consider future next time property purchases decision and new information methods. Hence, when one property consumer chooses to buy a house, it refers house features are house internal attributes , such as quality of building, the design as well as internal and external design, which are important factors for a property consumer when he/she needs to select and purchases one house.

The other (FM) factors which can influence the property consumers' needs, include living space as features, such as the size of kitchen, bathroom, bedroom, living bath and other rooms available in the house. The environment of housing area is also important factor, e.g. the condition of the hood, attractiveness of the area, quality of houses, type of houses, type of houses, density of housing, wooded area or free coverage, slope of the attractive views, open space, non-residential uses in the areas vacant sites, traffic noise, level of owner-occupation in , level of education in level of income in, security from crime, quality of schools, religious of , transportation , shopping center, sport entertainment can be supplied to close to the house area. All these human related issue of the property's location will also influence the property buyer's living location selection. Hence, above (FM) influence property consumer purchase behavior, it is based on the relationship behavior. The consumer's house purchase intention and house features, living space, environment and distance to recreation center, supermarket, library etc. public facilities variable (FM) factors.

In conclusion, the house internal space facility management and external environment facility management factors will influence property consumer individual house purchase intention.

● The effects of in-store shelf design facility management factor influences consumer behavior

Can every store retailer's shelf design influence supermarket and large retail stores shoppers' behaviors when they visit the stores? However, currently many stores tend to build on traditional and repetitive design for their store shelf layout, it brings results in outdated store layouts.

Another important store shelf layout design aspect, retailer should consider carefully is the allocation of products on shelves. So, it seems that efficient shelf space allocation management does not only minimize the economic threats of empty product shelves, it can also lead to higher consumer satisfaction, a better customer relationship.

Why does supermarket shelves design is important? Any retail tore will sell product category within a shelf. They can use the same nominal category , e.g. crisps next to light crisps, same food product shelf. Anyway, a goal-based shelf display can contain several product, that determine a common consumer goal, e.g. fair trade. Hence, these two categorical product structuring methods are also described in terms of how to put product, or food on shelf benefit and attribute -based product categories.

These shelf design food or product storing method will have more influence consumers to choose to buy the supermarket or retail store food or products more easily , due to products, or food put on their shelf very convenient and systematic to attract consumers' shopping consideration to the supermarket or retail store.

● Music (FM) environment influence consumer consumption desire

Is it possible that shop music (FM) environment can raise consumer purchase desire? In one shop or supermarket, it can provide soft music (FM) equipment to let consumers can listen soft music or songs in the supermarket or retail shop when the are staying to spend more time shopping and whether soft music facility can be expected to raise customer individual value-added options to the music facility shop in the supermarket or retail shop. Can the music facilities prolong consumers to stay in the store? It is possible that tempo soft music can influence consumers to stay longer time in restaurants and supermarkets and retail shops. It is possible that the different types of music (FM) in any supermarket, restaurant, retail shop owning music listening facility shopping environment. It will have possible to influence consumers to prolong staying in their shops. For example, one wine selling retail shop has classical music (FM) listening equipment to let consumers to listen when they enter the wine shop, it is possible to cause consumers to choose to buy more expensive wine products. Some researchers indicate when the wine shop owns classical music facility to let all consumers can list classical music when they walk in the wine ship, it can evoke the wine consumers to choose to buy purchasing higher prices wine products in the long term classical music listening environment. Otherwise, in a fitness sport center, musical fir and excite or popular music (FM) environment can attract fitness sport players' emotion to play and kind of fitness sport facility longer time. Also, in one supermarket, the soft music facilities listening environment can persuade or attract food consumers to spend more time in the mall consuming food or beverage also purchase other products more easily, due to they will listen soft music to be influenced to choose to prolong staying time in the supermarket. It seems that it has relationship between retail shop's music facility environment and consumer's emotion will be influenced by these different kinds of soft music or songs to raise consumption desire in the supermarket, if some consumers like to prolong to stay longer consuming time in the owning music facility environment's retail shop.

In fact, some researchers indicate the owning background music facility selling environment's ship , it can affect consumer decision making, memory, concentration consumption desire. So, classical , jazz soft music facility ought be installed in restaurants, retail shops, restaurants' environment. Otherwise, popular , exciting, noise, pop music facility ought be installed in fitness sport centers, theme park entertainment parks business places in order to influence fitness sport players or theme park entertainers to prolong playing or entertaining time to feel real sport or entertainment theme park playing machine facility's entertainment enjoyable feeling as well as attracting restaurant or supermarket or retail shop's consumers to prolong their staying time to make consumption decisions. Hence, it seems that music facility environment can raise consumers' consumption desire in possible.

● University bookstore atmospheric factors how to influence student's purchase book behavior?

Any university bookstore how to do international control and structuring of book internal environment to raise students' purchase book desires in university itself school's bookstore, it will be one popular question to any universities. Hence, whether the university bookstore internal (FM) factors include: lighting, music, colors, scents, temperature, layout and general cleanliness as well as university external factors include: the university bookstore shape/ size, windows, university parking facility for students availability and location, which can play an influential role of the university bookstore image in order to influence the university itself students to choose to buy books from themselves bookstore or university outside bookstores.

Whether the university student needs to spend how long individual learning time and how much learning nervous to spend time to choose any kinds of book in the universiity bookstore or outside bookstores, this issue , he/she will consider. Because he/she does want to expect spend much time and nervous to choose to buy books in any bookstore. If the university's bookstore physical location and internal (FM) image can let its target student customers to feel it's all book products are stored in any attractive internal book shelves places, e.g. the cheapest and the most expensive different subjects of text books are stored in one system method to bring the positive image of value and quality in order to let university target student customers can find their books' choice location to spend less time to search any books to read in the unviersiity bookstore easily.

However, due to learning time is shortage to every university student of the university's book shelves can display all text books in the attractive right locations in the university bookstore as well as the university's bookstore ought has an adequate space to let university students to walk to anywhere and find any subjects of text books and compare their book sale prices in the bookstore's any shelves' locations easily when they walk to the subject of book shelf location, then they can make accurate decision either to buy the right kind of subject book or not buy it to read in the short time. They will feel their book choice purchase decision making process won't influence their learning time in themselves universiity. Then, the university students will be influenced by themselves university's bookstore's attractive external university facilities in the university's any teaching places and the university's bookstore internal attractive environment facility image which can influence the students to make final choices to buy their liking books to read from their university's itself bookstore. Hence, the university's bookstore internal and external building environment (FM) design factors will influence its students whether choose to buy from themselves bookstore or another outside general bookstore.

● How and why does retail atmospheric environment influence consumers behavior in retail shop?

Any shop's internal facility management design can influence atmospheric environment to influence consumer individual shopping desire, e.g. colour, lighting, music, crowding, design and layout factors, which internal shop (FM) environment can influence the first time shopping visiting client ' cognitive process how to feel the shop store image. Such as if the store's (FM) environment can bring enjoyable and fun and happy image to let them to feel shopping's enjoyment.

In conclusion, when consumers will like to stay longer time in the store. Due to the store's internal (FM) atmospheric environment can attract them to stay longer time in the store. Then, the customer's shopping value will raise and it can bring purchasing intention and shopping satisfaction. How can (FM) influence retail atmospheric physical (FM) environment ? Can (FM) bring indirect relationship to influence how the consumer individual causes positive or negative purchase intention when he/she has influence to prolong staying desire in the store, when the shop has good (FM) , it will bring long time to make consumption chance in the shop.

● Facility management influences
consumer satisfactory service
level

Can facility management (FM) quality influence consumer satisfactory service feeling? Any organization's facility management can improve the effectiveness of the maintenance organization. It can provide improved operational and maintenance functions to maintain the physical environment to support the overall mission. However, any organization will consider whether it improves its facilities, it will raise consumer satisfactory feeling when it provides the service to them, e.g. education service industry, when students need to often to attend any school's classrooms or lecture halls, computer rooms, libraries, all these facilities will be student's learning environment. If these school facilities can be maintenance to let students to feel comfortable to enjoy to study in their schools' any learning locations. Then, it has possible that to bring their enjoyable learning feeling in theirs schools.

● How school's facility management influences student's learning satisfactory feeling.

However, in education industry case, the school's facility management has those criteria can be used to measure effectiveness. Student individual response time between the student's request for computer use service in school computer rooms, library reading service in school library , classroom computer facilities and tables, chairs etc. furniture supplies service and the facility management supply number and available to useful time. If the student believes that the response time is too long when he/she feels need to use any school facilities, the actual number of seconds or minutes, he/she needs to wait how long time to queue to use his/her school's any facilities in library, classroom, computer room. So, the student's queue waiting time to use any his/her school's facilities, it can measure the school's facility management effectiveness.

● Scheduling of preventive maintenance activities.

It schedules of any maintenance activities are not arranged effectively to the school. Then, it will influence students' poor learning facility service to their school. For their situation, when the school's first floor has two men toilets are damaged. They are needed to be required. However, it is one week period, the first floor 100 students can not use the first floor men toilets. Hence, in this week, all 100 students need to go to other floors toilets to often use. They will feel busy and time is not enough when they need to attend to any classrooms to listen the first floor classrooms teachers' lesson. If he/she arrives the first floor classroom too late, due to he/she needs to go to another floor male toilets to queue to use. Then, he/she will feel angry and worries about whose absent or late attending classroom behavior when the lesson's teacher has attended early in the first floor classroom , and he teacher will need him/her to explain why he/she will go to this classroom lately, if his/her explanation won't be accepted to attend to the first floor classroom too late in the week. So, arrangement maintenance schedule to any school's facilities issue is importnt to influence student's satisfactory feeling to the school. Also, lacking of preventive maintenance activities will bring results in unscheduled shutdown of critical equipment can have an unrecoverable impact on the school's good learning environment providing to student's mission.

In fact, however in any organizations, such as school, ship, office etc. organizations, achieving balance of effectiveness and efficient difficulties and takes time and effort on the part of management and staff. It is not enough to establish an optimal relationship between these two parts. It has another factor that organizations need to consider costs. In today's budget tightening environment, decreasing expenses requires accepting a lower level of efficiency and effectiveness. The goal is to determine the point at which decreasing efficiency and effectiveness is no longer acceptable before that point is reached.

It brings this question : How to apply facility management knowledge to rise efficiency and effectiveness in order to improve quality standard of service to satisfy consumers' needs in short time? Such as school's facilities service case. What factors can influence student's level of satisfaction with regards to higher educational facilities services? It seems that any school's facilities will influence its students how to satisfy its education service indirectly. Because they need often to go to school to learn. So, any school's facilities, e.g. classrooms, computer rooms, libraries, toilets, lecture halls, canteens, sport and entertainment centers, research laboratories, school car parks, student enquiry counters, all these places to the school's any students will attend. So, how raise schools' facilities improvement to satisfy students' learning needs in the school's any locations which will have help to influence it student individual satisfaction level to the school's service, instead of every teacher individual teaching performance service to the school's students.

For any service organizations , such as hotels, restaurant, financial institutions, retail stores and hospitals etc. The physical environment can influence how customers' evaluation of their service. Due to service has intangible nature, so customers will rely on evaluate service quality.

Any higher education institutions are education service providing organizations. They need have comfortable and enjoyable educational environment to be provided to the students to attend the school's any places in order to meet whose learning expectations and studying experience needs. So, the school's facility management will be one factor to influence student's learning satisfaction when they expect to attend the school's any locations or places to let them to feel the school's learning environment have good facility management feeling.

In fact, if the school has comfortable classrooms or lecture halls educational environment to let its students to feel, it will bring assistance to raise their learning satisfactory feeling. So, comfortable learning facility management environment is one kind of school's facility service characteristics, it includes intangibility, perishability, inseparability and variability. So, they are every student individual learning feeling when they are attending to the school's any learning locations. So, school's facility management service feeling will influence whether they expect to choose this school to study. If the school's facility management learning environment is more comfortable and teaching facilities are better to compare other schools' facilities. Then, it will have possible to attract many students to choose this school to study. Such as any educational organizations, instead of the teachers (lecturers and professors) whose educational level is influence students number. The university's building environment will influence students' learning feeling, when they attend in the university. The facilities include laboratories, lecture theatres an offices, but also residential accommodations, catering facilities, sports and recreations centers because university students need have university life feeling to let them to fell the university can give welfare services , e.g. medical services, career guidance, sport entertainment, residential accommodation etc. service, instead of educational learning service in classrooms and lecture theatres. Hence, university's diversification facilities services are needed to satisfy university students to choose it to study, instead of university teacher's educational performance.

When one student can enroll the university to study from secondary education institution. The admitted student will usually consider two aspects to decide to choose the university to study. One aspect is the academic programs, of sequence of courses choices and the another aspect is the university's facilities whether they can satisfy their university life need, e.g. library, dorms, bookstore, food canteen , gym's sport entertainment, education technological facilities in the classrooms and lecture theatres to let the students to feel the university's teaching facilities are achieved his/her learning demand.

So, these two factors (teaching and learning and facilities) are linked to each other to influence student's total school learning experience and attitude towards a particular institution and this is termed as value chain in the student's learning process in the university. Hence, student individual evaluation variables will include teaching staff, teaching method, enrolment and facility enough supply actual service need.

However, the university's facilities, such as any residential accommodation, canteen, library , classroom, lecture theatre, sport gym, entertainment center will be their useful facilities need to satisfy their learning, entertainment and eating ,even living need in residential accommodation in the school's learning life experience every day. If one student chooses to live in the university residential accommodation . All of his/her learning and eating and living time and spending will be calculated to the university's any facilities to let him/her to feel it can provide enough facilities to let him/her to enjoy.

Hence, the facility management factor, such as overall campus environment, library, laboratory, classroom, lecturer theatre size and facility supply of on campus accommodation, welfare right service, parking areas, cafeteria , sport center etc. They will be every students facilities service needs from the university supplies choice. So, any university ought not neglect how to improve itself university's space area facilities to achieve satisfy their needs after they choose this university to study. Hence, any university's facility management will influence how the student's satisfactory learning service feeling when he/she chooses the university to study.

In conclusion, better facility management will attract more students to choose the university to study. Otherwise, worse facility management will not attract more students to choose to study the school. Hence, it seems that the school's facility management factor has relationship to influence student's satisfactory feeling, instead of teacher individual teaching performance factor to the school.

● Property facility management influences householder buying behavior

One new property's low price is attractive factor to influence property buyer individual preference choice. Does the new individual's facility management factor influence the property buyer's preference choice decision, if the property buyer feels its facility management is better than other similar properties, even it's price is higher than other properties. I shall indicate some cases to analyze this possibility as below:

Some properties' facility management service quality has possible to create true value for any property buyers when they consider the calculation ingredients to make decision whether to new property has higher value to choose to buy. The factors may include: price, natural environment, transportation tools convenient available, shopping centers supplies, the neighour quality, and the property's internal facility management etc. factors.

In fact, car or house purchase buyers, they have similar behaviors. It is that car's buyers will consider the car's machines whether they are safe to drive on roads, instead price, manufacture loyalty factors. It is possible that the car's machines quality factor will be preference to any car buyers when they make preference decisions to choose which brand its cars are the suitable. However, if the car's brand is famous and its appearance beautiful and price is cheap. But the car consumer feels its machine qualities are unsafe to let the driver to drive on road. Then, the car's poor machine quality factor will influence the car buyer's decisions to choose to buy this car. It can influence the car buyer individual car purchase decision.

The car buyer's behavior is similar to property buyer's behavior. Although, the new property price is cheap, good neigh ours are living near to the new property's location, shopping centers and transportation tools are available to near to this new property's area. But if the property buyers' feels its facility management is poor quality to compare other similar properties. Then, the poor quality of facility management factor will have possible to influence the property buyers whose final buying decision to choose to buy this new property. It brings this question: How and why can the facility management poor quality factor influence property consumers' preference choice?

In general, all property consumers won't know whether the new property's facility management is good or bad quality , they need to spend time to visit to the new property in order to observe whether its internal facility is satisfactory to his/her acceptable level. In simple, their purchase decision will regard to how to allocate household budget, how the household's economic resources are influenced, e.g. for travelling, visits to restaurants, comparing the different similar types of property product groups, e.g. apartments or houses or houses of a givn size data. For example, if one property's room(s) size is (re) small to compare other kind similar product type of room(s) size. Although the prior property's price is cheaper to compare to the later properties. But, if some property buyers hoped the property has large room(s) size, then the later larger room(s) size which will be possible to some property buyer's preference choice. Even, their property price is more expensive to compare the smaller room(s) size of properties. Thus, the property's room size which will be one major factor to influence property buyers' purchase decision. room's size had relationship to facility management issue. Moreover, if the room's quality and design is attractive, then it will bring more attractive to persuade some property buyers to choose to buy them to live in preference.

Hence, whether the new property is good durable product feeling which will influence householder's choice. If the householder feels the new property has long term durable life to avoid to spend much maintenance expense when they have been living in the new property for a long term period. They will believe it has better facility management, quality to let them to live longer time and the most importance is that they do not need to spend any maintenance expense , due to the property 's any internal facilities are damaged easily.

The external factors may include: culture, reference groups, family, social class and demography of lifestyle as well as internal factors may include: feelings, past property buying and living experience , property knowledge, motivation of the property buyer individual psychology. These both factors can influence any property buyer individual decision making process to do final house purchase behavior. However, internal factors, such as: property knowledge of facility management and property living experience, e.g. how to evaluate to choose to buy the property , due to the property buyer's past living experience for the past property's facilities whether its facilities can satisfy its property buyers' comfortable living needs. This internal factor will be more important to influence any property buyer's property purchase final decision. If he/she feels whose prior old property's facilities are satisfactory. Then, he/she will compare this new property and old property's facilities to decide whether this new property is value to buy. So, the old property's facility will be the measurement standard to compare his/her next new property purchase choice. So, the property purchaser will compare these new and old property's property facilities product knowledge to similarities among property alternative which will influence his/her final decision to choose to buy the new property to live.

It seems that property low price factor must not guarantee to attractive many property buyers' choice. Otherwise, it is assumed that many property buyers like rent or buy to live the property for themselves for long term intention. There are less property buyers expect to sell the first property to earn profit intention. So, they will usually consider whether the property is long term durable product to avoid to pay maintenance expense when they had been living in the property in long term.

Some factors that taking consideration are proximity to the specific location, housing prices, developer's brand, the payment scheme, reference group, which are not the main factors to influence any property buyer individual choice. Because property buyer's need is that the property has good facilities to supply to them to live, e.g. good heater equipment can provide hot water to them to bath in winter or good air conditioners can provide cold temperature to let them to feel cool comfortable feeling in summer in their homes. Good electric tools facilities , when they have need to use electricity in safe environment at home, e.g. car park accessibility facility , level of security facility , surface area facility and housing types, bedroom, bathroom facilities, quality of housing manufacturing raw material, house design , house durable guarantee, speed of complaint responsiveness, specification accuracy, confirmation of building plan service, showing legal file property purchase process service, finance instalments process assistance, speed of responsiveness, officers' skills of presentation. All of above these concern property facility management issues will influence any property buyers' final choice to decide whether the property is value to buy. So, facility management will influence property purchaser individual final decision in possible.

● Hotel facilities influence hotel consumer choice

Travellers choose hotel to live. They will consider price, room comfortable feeling, hotel location , gum sport or entertainment service facility supplies , hotel room booking service etc. factors to decide whether the hotel can achieve every traveller individual minimum living need. However, whether hotel facilities factor will be the main factor to influence travellers' living needs. How and why do travellers consider hotel facilities whether are enough supply or facilities of quality to satisfy their demand to cause their living choice to the hotel final decision.

Usually, hotel's customers won't plan to live too long time, e.g. more than three months in the hotel. Because they are travelling aim. It will bring this question: Does hotel facilities quality consider to influence their hotel living choice if the traveller is short-term traveller to the country? However , some travellers who have effort to spend money to live high class hotels, even their journey is short trip. Hence it seems that short trip , hotel living reason can not influence the high class hotel travellers' living comfortable demand to the high class hotel room. Hence , the high class hotel room's facility management quality is also needed high performance. Even, when they need to eat breakfast, lunch , dinner in the high class hotel canteens or playing any sport equipment, or gum equipment or wathching movie in the hotel's small cinema room . They must need high class hotel can supply more entertainment, restaurant , sport facilities to satisfy their comfortable needs in the high class hotel. Moreover, they must consider safety issue when they are living in the high class hotel. So, thy must demand the hotel have enough five fright equipment in their rooms, or corridors and the stairs to let them can leave the dangerous locations to arrive the most safe locations immediately when the hotel has fire accident occurrence in any where . So, it ensures that the high class hotel's customers must ensure the high class hotel's facilities can satisfy their any one of above these needs before they decide to live this high class hotel.

In fact, high class hotel's room price must be more expensive to compare the low class hotel. So, it explains why high class hotel's consumers will need the hotel has safe and good quality of facilities to let them to feel it is one reasonable price, safe , good service and good facilities' high class hotel to live. Usually, when the traveller arrives the country to travel, the travelers chooses the hotel to live, it is whose first time visit in common. So, he/she ought consider that the hotel environment seems it is good or bad to let the traveller to select to live. If the hotel's facility environment is new and beauty and design colorful to let the first time travellers to feel. Then, it is possible that good facilities environment can influence the first time travellers to select to live, even the hotel's room price is more expensive to compare other similar hotels in the travelling living places. Hence, it explains why hotel facilities can influence traveller individual room booking choice. When he/she is the first time to visit the hotel to select whether to live or not.

● How and why facility management can influence workplace productivity to bring customer satisfaction

Facility management is one part of manufacturers or retailers as their productivity in workplace as their input and functionalistics within physical environment. In fact, facility management in workplace may include: site selection, property disposal, site acquisition, workplace space allocation, space inventory, space forecasting facility management, interior furniture change planning, interior furniture installation, moving maintenance, inventory, design evaluation, employment satisfaction evaluation plan, external maintenance and breakdown maintenance, preventive maintenance, landscape maintenance, energy space facility management, hazardous waste disposal, capital , operating furniture budgeting. So, it seems that one workplace considered whether the workplace's facility is enough to let employees to work in order to raise efficiency and improve productive performance more easily. Then, it will bring this question:

● How and why workplace facility management can influence consumer individual satisfaction?

Strategic FM delivery is essential for business survival. I shall explain why for delivery is important to influence customer satisfaction. In business process view point, an effective and meaningful service to their customer , i.e. the user. For logistic industry, the product's delivery time will influence when the product can be sent to the user's arrival destination. If the product is delayed to sent to the user's home or office or any location destination. The reason is because the logistic product sender has no efficient facility management (FM) arrangement in its warehouse . Then, its warehouse lacks efficient (FM), which will cause users to feel its delivery service is poor and they will complain its delivery service staffs. Then, they will find another delivery service company to replace its service. So, it explains that logistic industry's warehouse (FM) service arrangement can raise efficient time to send any products to their customers in order to let they feel satisfactory service. For example, Amazon online logistic company's warehouse has applied artificial intelligence robotic tools to assist warehouse workers to arrange the different kinds of products to deliver to the right shelves . Then, the warehouse robotics will follow their right product shelves locations to follow the right products to deliver to US domestic or overseas product buyers in the short time and it can avoid the wrong products to deliver to the wrong buyers' risk. Also, the (AI) delivery tools can raise time efficiency to assist Amazon warehouse workers to reduce their work load, and tried to work in large warehouse environment. Although, its warehouse's area is large, the (AI) tools facility can help them to deliver the different products to different shelves in the right locations , e.g. exact product number and the kinds of product to be delivered to the right country' client's shelf location in the warehouse. Also, it implies FM is very important to influence Amazon warehouse delivery efficiency and avoiding delivery wrong occurrence chance. For example, the shelf location belongs to US domestic customers, or the shelf location belongs to Japan customers, or the shelf location belongs to Hong Kong customers, or any other Asia or Western countries' different customers' locations. The warehouse's facility needs have different countries' shelves enough space to put and it also need enough space to let the (AI) tools, robotic delivery workers and human workers both to walk to different shelves locations easily and the different countries' shelves number needs to be calculated accurate. For example, it has how many client number will buy Amazon's the kind product per day. If it has above 5,000 to 10,000 China clients to buy the kind of product. Then, it will need to make judgement how many shelves are placed in the warehouse. So, it can avoid to lack enough shelves to put any different kinds of products to prepare to delivery to China clients in efficient time and it won't avoid to delay to deliver to their homes or offices or any locations in China. Hence, such as Amazon logistic case, it explains why warehouse's space shelves number and area or locations facility management can influence workers or (AI) delivery tools how to move convenient and avoiding the delivery to the customer's wrong destination chance occurrence and shortening time to deliver products to its clients efficiently. Then, due to the delivering time is shorten and the wrong delivery destination's occurrence chance is also reduced , even it can avoid to deliver the product to wrong client's destination occurrence. Then, the logistic firm's clients will feel more satisfactory to its product sale delivery service and their complaints will be avoided. Hence, it explains effective warehouse (FM) space management service arrangement is essential to any logistic businesses nowadays.

● Facility management brings departmental benefits

Why do organizations need have facility management (FM) service? As above examples indicate that (FM) can improve workplace environment facilities, e.g. warehouse environment to let workers to raise efficiencies or improve performances, even it can influence consumers to raise satisfactory to it's services indirectly, also it can help organizations' equipment to be used long term to cause old and are needed to spend expenditure to maintenance or change new equipment in order to improve better quality . So , it can assist organizations to avoid to spend more expenditure for new equipment purchase or maintenance. All these issues will be facility management service's benefits to an organizations, which can concern raising customers' service satisfaction, raising efficiency or improving productive performance, raising productivity, reducing equipment or property maintenance or new alternation much of expenditure spending, office or warehouse or any workplace space planning arrangement .

However, every organization will need a facility manager or manage whose team effectively . When a facility manager begins to apply FM techniques to solve business problems. The case for FM is made.

It is a simple matter of demonstrating a qualified return on the investment required. Every organization's success, FM operation of three key activities: they include: needing a proper understanding of the organization's needs, wants, drivers and goals and knowing when needs to review its changing circumstances, developing an effective facilities solution o support the organization's needs, wants , property drives and contribute to achieve its goals both short term and long term, achievement of reliable delivery of that solution in a managed, measured manner.

So, it bring one question: What are the influential factors to be followed the right direction to FM manager's strategic FM operational decision? The influencing factors may include: ownership, governance sector, complexity and perhaps of most significant, the size of the organization's property portfolio.

In fact, major occupiers feel FM service need, they are large corporate organizations and public service organizations. Their aims usually are to raise. The most marginal improvement in efficiency or effectiveness, these aims are the great significance. Major property occupiers will already have a facilities department or individuals performing the FM function with another department like property, finance or human resource, sale and marketing's facilities.

Usually these FM need occupiers who will encounter this problem: How can apply FM service systems and processes to be developed to improve reliable service delivery making use of the economies of scale, not suffering because of the size of the problem. This question will be facility manager individual concerning question: How to apply (FM) technique to solve the improvement reliable service delivery making use of the economics of scale problem for whose organization?

In reality much of external facilities management benefits to organizations, instead of raising efficiency, improving performance, raising productivity, reducing maintenance expenditure, e.g. energy saving, reducing natural resource waste, increasing local employment, improving supply chain management are all elements of the FM contribution to every organization's need. Hence are the work life balance argument and provision of an effective and safe working environment that supports why some organizations feel need (FM) service to support their organizational development.

Moreover, on cost benefit of space saving efficient view point, space service cost reduction is a key driver for all organizations and the medium, or large sized players will benefit directly from a well coordinated facilities strategy. For example, application FM technique to help warehouse or office space area to save 50% space vacancy to let employees can move easily or putting enough furniture or equipment or many stocks can be putted in warehouses . So, paying more rent expenditure to rent or purchasing another new warehouse or office to satisfy workers or employees' working environment to be better need. If the organization has effective (FM) technique, then it has enough space vacancy to supply to the increase stocks number to be putted inside in warehouse and it can let workers to move safety in available to let staffs to move easily and equipment have enough space to be stored in the limited warehouse space problem.

For greater space savings benefits will bring either long term renting or buying of increasing offices or warehouse number expenditure problem to any organizations, when the organizations' cost or renting or buying accommodation probably accounting for 60 to 70% of total occupancy cost . So a strategic program to release space or the prevent the acquisition of moves can be the most significant consideration to any facility manager, with between 40% and 60% of the workplaces are unoccupied in most offices or warehouses at any given moment in time.

Hence, how to apply (FM) technique to save space occupied areas for employment moving or stocks or equipment saving need in offices or warehouses. This issue will be any facility managers' seeking methods to solve problem. However, the important major advantage of facility management to organizations is that the application of management principle to keep the organization's property assets with the aim of maximizing their potentials. Thus, any organizations' facilities have become important, due to the property facilities' worth will increase if the organization's facility management technique can protect the organization's facilities have good performance. Then, the organization's maintenance expenditure will reduce and it won't need to spend expenditure to buy any new facilities to replace old facilities , due to they often damage factor when they are used old.

In conclusion, it explains why effective FM combines resources and activities can raise work environment improvement, which is essential to the raising employee performance aim. For hotel living service case example, this industry must need have good facility management service because hotels must need to fully equipped in term and facilities for effectiveness to satisfy hotel living clients' demand , hotels ought need good facilities asset management style lead to effectiveness in service delivery, there are benefit derivable from the adoption of facilities management from which other hotels can learn from for their effective operations. Hence, it explains why effective FM can bring benefits to hotels' properties to be more comfortable, beautiful appearances to attract many hotel customers to choose to live the hotel. Because hotel's building industrial kitchens, rooms facilities, equipment , halls of categories, restaurant facilities, gum sport entertainment centers' facilities, fans, elevators, lifts, electrical installation, escalators, baking equipment, recreational facilities, including golf courses which will be important factors to influence hotel clients' comfortable living feeling, if the hotel can keep its all facilities in the best living environment often. Then, it can raise chance to attract many hotel customers to choose it to live. So , hotel industry has absolute need to implement effective FM strategy to keep its properties more attractive to satisfy its clients' living needs.

Instead of hotel industry, logistic transportation industry also needs effective facilities management in warehouse, because of the logistic company's warehouse 's facilities are good, then it will assist to raise employee individual efficiency in the safe and system shelve stored facilities in workplace environment and improving performance.

Consequently, it will bring the shorten time to deliver any products to clients to avoide the delaying time delivery in order to let customers to feel more satisfactory to their services. In simple, it seems that some industries need have effective facilities management techniques to help them to bring long term customer satisfactory feeling, worker individual efficiency raising and performance improvement benefits. Hence, it seems facility management techniques' demand will be increased to some industries in popular in the future because it has help to raise employee individual efficiency , productive performance and client individual satisfactory level consequently.

● How to impact of workplace
management on well-being and
productivity

In facility management strategy, design can lead promotion, the value of offices that are enriched, particularly including warehouses, shopping centers to raise their market value. Moreover, effective organizations, such as raising powering workers when giving the effective design of office space. I assume that a good design of an interior office workspace environment seems a psychological department to influence staff individual emotion to bring positive power in order to raising productive efficient influence, such as in a commercial city office. So, it brings this question: How workspace management strategy can impact on staff's working behaviors in office.

In fact, office tasks general include various forms of productivity, e.g. information processing, information management and any clerical tasks by computerization. Hence, office productivity concerns how to influence each office white color worker applies computers to work in office. The office space can impact on white color workers' performances in these several aspects: feeling of psychological comfort, organizational physical comfort and job satisfaction and productivity, efficiency. So, it seems that office workspace design strategy can influence white color workers' working behavior and attitude and performance indirectly.

The office space management includes: how to removal from the workspace of everything except the materials required to do the job at hand, how tight managerial control of the workspace, and how to implement standardization of managerial practice and workspace design. So, these key ideas will influence how each white color worker's efficiency and productivity in office working environment.

For this office space design situation, a large unseparated small space size's space design can accommodate more people and so brings itself to economies of scale. As a result, space occupancy can be centrally managed with minimal disruptive interference from office workers. Indeed, many businesses now adopt a clean and fresh air office working policy because they have more employees than they have spaces at which they can work. This desks are either taken on a first -come first -served basis. (hot desking) or can be booked in advance. So , when a company has many employees need to work in a small space working environment. It must concern how to let staffs to feel more comfortable in order to reduce high psychological pressure to work in this uncomfortable working environment. Hence, it explains why workspace design can impact on office workers' performance in some offices. All these issues are assumed that empowering workers to manage and have input into the design of their own workspace, then the effective office or any working places space management will enhance wellbeing to bring workers' positive emotions and improving productivity. I also assume the space working environment design have relationship of these depend variable factors to influence office worker individual productive efficiency. The variable factors may include psychological comfort, organizational comfortable, job satisfaction, physical comfort and productivity.

However, office furniture , facilities will influence office white color workers' performance ,e.g. the room size whether is big or small for manage office worker, a high backed, comfortable leather chair is needed for office staffs to sit down to let more comfortable, the door and most of the walls need glass, the office room environment needs have sea-grass rug beneath the desk covering the immediate working area, the office also needs have plants and pictures, mail boxes, telephone and computer facility is needed. When one staff needs to send email or phone call or send letters or deliver documents conveniently. These office elements are essential in order to increase physical well-being and feeling of satisfaction to white-color workers. Hence, geren office and office working space design management is needed in order to influence white color workers' productive efficiency in long term.

● **Effective workspace design can influence communication to raise productivity**

Office white-color workers often need communication between their managers, supervisors, and themselves. Office communication extends from the way that a user experiences a service. An effective office communication can bring these benefits; Providing positive influence on decision making by presenting a strong point of view and developing mutual understanding, delivering efficient decisions and solutions by providing accurate , timely and relevant information, enabling mutually benefit solutions, building health relationships by encouraging trust and understanding between the high level, middle level and low level staffs.

Effective office communication needs to clearly communicate its nature and purpose. Good communication ensures that all service staffs are sending out the same messages. Communication is also important for ensuring the service understands what users requires and why he/she talks about understanding users' needs and communication receiver can have effective communication skill to understand what he/she needs the another to do and the another knows he/she ought how to work by his/her task demand. Then, it will shorten much time. If the office has 100 staffs need to often communicate. However, if the office has good space management arrangement to let every staff can communicate easily and walks to anywhere to find the right staff to communicate conveniently. Then, they can spend less time to waste on communication issue. Then, their productive efficiency will be also influence to raise.

● Health and safe work environment influences productivity

Is a health and safe work environment can raise employees' work productive efficiencies indirectly? How and why it can influence employees' productive performance? Some occupations' working environments are easier to occur occupational accidents and diseases risks when the workers are working in the high health and safe risk's working environment. Hence, health and safety issues at these high life risk workplaces can be considered as a key to influence employees' overall performance. The idea that health and safety management program have positive impacts on productivity. When one worker needs to work in this high risk of health and safe workplace. He/she will consider whether how his/her work behavior will bring suffer serious injuries for shorter or longer time from work related causes in possible. So, he/she will work carefully in order to avoid injuries occurrence chance. It is possible to influence whose work performance, low productive efficiency in order to avoid any occupational accident occurrences in the dangerous workplace.

If the employee feels danger when he/she needs to stay in the warehouses stable location to work often. Then his/her absenteeism day number will have increase, due to he/she feels that workplace accidents and occupational illnesses and can lead to permanent occupational disability, when he/she needs to attend the stable dangerous workplace to work in the warehouse. Hence, he/she will choose to apply holiday often in order to avoid injuries chance increasing when he/she needs to stay in the stable workplace location in the warehouse. It explains why companies increase need qualified, motivated and efficient workers who are able willing to contribute activity to technical and organizational innovations. So, healthy workers working in healthy working conditions are thus an important precondition for organization to work smoothly and productively. Hence, a health and safety workplace environment can bring these benefits to organizations as below:

It can prevent among workers of learning work, due to health problems caused by their working conditions, the protection of workers in their employment from risks resulting from factors adverse to health. The placing and maintenance of the worker in an occupational, environment adapted to his/her physiological and psychological, capabilities, mental , physical and social conditions of workplace and adequacy of health and safety measures are needed to any employees in order to bring positive impact not only on safety and health performance, but also productivity. However, identifying and quantifying these effects will difficult to be measured as well as the quality of a working environment has a strong influence on productive efficiency.

For one aviation air plane manufacturing factory, where workplace can environment will have high risk to occur occupational related accidents to cause employees' injuries. Hence, employees will be consider themselves safety when they need to work in high accident occurrence workplace. The bad consequence will influence such as absenteeism day number increases, leaving this kind of aviation air plane job of employees number increases, low productive efficiencies, due to there are many proficient experienced employees who choose leave this kind of high accident risk occupation.

Consequently, any high accident occurrence risk workplace environment , employers need have good safe and health strategy to let their employees have confidence to work in this kind of high risk accident occurrence workplace if they expect low productive efficiencies effect is caused by high accident occurrence risk workplace factor.

● Employee personal
empowerment factor influences
performance
Is empowerment one good method to raise employee himself/

herself effort in order to improve productive efficiency in organizations. Empowerment often consists of support groups, e.g. management's effective leading or trainer's training, course educational opportunities. Employee self-management education may impact to improve himself/herself job performance, e.g. increased self-empowerment, self-management skills and job treatment satisfaction.

Only organization's empowerment strategy can lead every employee to through improvements in the employee individual decision making efficacy, improvement task performance behavior by reviewing whether what are the employee himself/herself errors when he/she encounters any job difficulties, after he/she reviewed his/her task error and his/her manager feels his/her performance can be improved. Then, it can enhance satisfaction with the employee and his/her manage relationship and better access and raising efficient performance in possible . Hence, empowerment can let every employee to discover whether what task related difficulties he/she faces or encounters every day. When his/her manager give ideas to let him/her to know how he/she ought review his/her task error in a supportive education working environment, it aims to let the low performance or low inefficient employees to increase confidence to continue work in the organization. So, the employee turnover number will decrease , if the inefficient employees can feel that they can attempt to solve their task-related difficulties successfully by themselves. So, empowerment can increase social support, leadership and advocacy development , it has resulted in greater employee individual performance psychological empowerment, autonomy and authority to let every employee to feel to achieve to improve themselves efficiencies more effectively in any organizations.

For hospital organizational efficiency measurement empowerment influence case, how empowerment can influence hospital's efficiency raising? Efficiency is one of the most important indicators of hospital performance evaluation. Why do some hospitals' efficiencies poor? It is possible that mis management of resources, lacking health plan packages, e.g. coverage of basic health insurance, poor quality of care service, more payment demand for out-of pocket payment , quality of primary healthcare , healthcare providers neglect to concern potentially about service efficiency issues.

In fact, low hospital efficiency is the major problem to influence patients number to choose the hospital's medical service, e.g. when the hospital often needs patients to queue to wait for doctor's care medical service. They need to wait on hour at least or more when the hospital has many patients are waiting for its medical service. Then, it will influence them to choose another hospital to replace it , if the hospital 's medical fee is cheaper and it does not need patients to spend long time to queue to wait its medical service. So, service efficiency is important to influence patients consumers' positive or negative feeling to choose the hospital's medical service. Even, the hospital's doctors are famous or they own many medical working experience, if patients often need long time to queue to wait its medical service . Then, it will cause its patients number to be reduced .

These are variable factors to influence the hospital's inefficiency. They may include old speed hospital information system and medical record documents based on inefficient input and output variables. Input variables may include the number of hospital admissions, the number of nurses and the number of available beds. The output variable may include average of length of stay and bed turnover interval inefficient paper document record in the patient record administrative department.

However, to evaluate the hospital efficiency indicators may include technical, scale and managerial efficiency the out-based data development analysis approach and the variable returns to scales assumption was used. Based on the out-input based approach (maximizing the factors of medical service production), to increase efficiency the organization should be increased outputs.

Hence, when the hospital has good efficient evaluation method to measure every staff's performance , e.g. ward administrative clerk, patient registration clerk etc. Then, it can base on an put-put based approach and assuming a variable return to scale, there is capacity to improve technical efficiency and managerial efficiency in these any hospital different administrative units without an increase in costs and use of same amount of resources in relation to technical efficiency and managerial efficiency and scale efficiency of hospital's administrative labour individual task.

In conclusion, factors, such as modification of managerial practices, use of modern technologies tailored to the cultural, political and formulation of clinical guidelines to standardize the medical processes in order to reduce medical errors and increase the empowerment of health care buyers (insurance organizations), length of stay, management hospitals by specialist managers, administrative requirement, full time hospital physicians, limiting the authority of decision makers in relation to the recruitment of staff in accordance with the needs of the hospital and optimal allocation of beds, conducting economic evaluations and the type of hospitals ownership had an impact on the hospital efficiency significantly. By increasing the number of beds the hospitals efficiency decreases. Otherwise, optimizing the bed size can increase hospital efficiency.

However, the important factor to raise hospital overall staffs efficiencies empowerment is needed to let every hospital staff to review whether why and how himself/herself error is caused and he/she needs to review his/her errors to avoid to be caused from any negligence again in order to avoid patients' complaints again or reduce the patients' complaint number aims. So, empowerment of staff himself/herself error review factor is one major raising efficient good method.

● facility management influences the new employees
production efficiencies

In psychological view ,in any organization's environments, they depend on the types of social and physical environment factors to influence employee personal behavior how to be caused. How and why does the employee select to do whose behavior? If the organization's physical and social environment is better, then it may influence its employees select to work hard. It is possible to bring productive efficient raising consequence.

In fact, when one new employee enters the new organization to work, he/she needs to learn how to adapt to cooperate with the organization's old employees to work together. So, it explains how and why organization's physical and social environment can influence the new employee individual motivation of behavior to work. In regarding new employee individual behavior by new employer's culture expectations as well as new employees need to adapt of actions that are likely to productive positive outcomes and generally discard those that bring unrewarding or puniishing outcomes by new employer's treatment.

However, anticipated material and organization environment co-operation outcomes between the new employee and the organization old employees' cooperation, which are not the only kind of incentives that influence the new employee behavior of the new employee actions were performed only on behalf of anticipated external rewards and punishment from the new employer. In actuality, the new employee concerns considerable self-direction in the face of the new employer's organization's old employees competing influences. However, when the new employee has adopted an intension and an action plan. When, he/she works in the new organization for a period, he/she can't simply not back and visit for the appropriate performances to appear.

The new employee's new job goal will be motivated by enlisting self-evaluative engagement in activities rather than directly. By making self-evaluation conditional on matching personal new job standards, the new employee will give direction to his/her new job pursuits and create self-inventions to sustain his/her efforts for new job goal attainment. The new employee will select to do new task behavior to give him/her self-satisfaction and a sense of pride and self worth for the new job chance.

Efficacy beliefs also play a key role in shaping the new employees' behavior to do their tasks by influencing the types of new organization's activities and working environments, the new employees choose to set into any factor that influences the employee's choice behavior can affect the direction of employee personal career development in the new organization. This is because the organizational working environment influences operating in the employee how to select working environments continue to work. Thus, by choosing and shaping the new organization's working environments, new employee can have a hand in what they expect.

In conclusion , when a new employee chooses the new organization to work. He/she must need to adapt the organization's new working environment. If he/she feels difficult to adapt or accept to the organization's new working environment, then he/she will be influenced to work inefficient or poor productive performance , due to he/she feels unhappy to work the new organization's working environment and the new organization's manager will dissatisfy his/her performance and complain or give verbal warning to dismiss him/her. Then, it will bring the poor consequence to let the organization's inefficient productive performance effect. If many new employees feel difficult to adapt to work in the new organization. Then, inefficient productive performance will be influenced to keep a long term. So, it implies that the organization will need to change its organizational culture in order to let many new employees can adapt and accept this new organizational culture to work happily if the organization expects new employees work to raise productive efficiency successfully.

● Raising efficient and effective
interview psychological methods

In human resource department, interviewing and selecting the most right applicants to do different kinds of positions, it is one part of HRM function. If the interviewer need to spend more time to interview to decide whom is the most right applicant to do the position in one day, e.g. 50 at least , even more applicants number as well as he/she can also make the more accurate personal selection decision to choose the most right applicant to do the position after the interview day. Then, the interviewing process needs to be avoided to spend more time to choose the most suitable applicant to do the position within the day. It is difficult to judge whether whom ought be the most right applicant to do the position, if there are more than 50 applicants , they are needed to be interview in the day. The consequence will bring HR department can spend extra time to do the interview task, but it can have enough staffs and time and resource to do other urgent or important task at the interview day. It will bring this question: How to apply psychological method to raise interviewer's efficiency to shorten to spend extra time to do interviewing tasks ? I shall explain some psychological methods to attempt to let interviewers have more confidence to select the most right applicant in short time as below:

1. Behavioral interview skill

The interviewer can apply the actual behavioral interview method to let the interviewee to answer how he/she deals the matters, he/she feels that it is the best decision in order to judge and analyze whether whom applicant is the most suitable to be selected, e.g. describing the situation, he/she needs or the task that he/she needs to accomplish. The situation may be from a previous job, any relevant event, describing the action he/she took and be sure to keep the focus on him/her , e.g. discussing a group project or effort in the team; explaining what results he/she achieved, what happen? How did the event and what dis the applicant accomplishes? What did the applicant learn?

In the behavioral-based interview. the interviewer can need the applicant to attempt to explain examples clearly in order to judge whose analytical skill whether he/she is the suitable applicant to do the position. The interviewer may ask the applicant to identify some examples from whose post experience where he/she demonstrated top behaviors and skills that employers typically seek. To judge whether his/her examples should be totally positive, such as accomplishments or meeting goals, the other half should be situations that started at negatively , but either ended positively or he/she made the best of the outcome.

This behavioral interview test aims to review whether the applicant's every example answer, he/she can provide an appropriate description of how he/she demonstrated the desired behaviors. In the behavioral interview, the interviewer can attempt to judge whether the applicant has good imagine effort to mind any relatively small set of examples to respond to a number of different behavioral questions to satisfy the right example are applied to the right situations in the limited interview time. Hence, behavioral interview can let the interviewer to make more accurate analysis to judge whether whom applicant(s) has (have) good analytical effort to solve any work-related situational problems in the most reasonable way or attitude in order to select whom is the most right applicant to do the position.

2. E-mail interviewing in qualitative research

E-mail interviewing is another good interview method to select right applicant to do the managerial level position. E-mail interviewing can be in many cases a viable alternative to face-to-face telephone interviewing. Internet-based qualitative research methods may include online personal interview and virtual focus groups. However, it brings two questions: What opportunities and challenges does online in depth interviewing present for collectively qualitative data? How can in depth e-mail interviews be conducted effectively?

The applicant targets may be the top-level manager, advertising executive , sales manager, human resource manager etc. management position applicants. They need to answer any complex or difficult interviewing question by email in the limited time, e.g. how to solve one case study problem , how to give recommendation to solve the situation problem. The interview participants may be recruited by tool/method of psychological test questions, the interview questions may be interview guide in a single e-mail and follow yp, length of email data collection period may be up to

10 weeks, the number of e-mail or follow up exchanges may be several number. The electronic formal and require little editing or formation before the applicants are processed for analysis all e-mail interviewing questions. So, they need to answer any managerial case study problem in limited time.

It is one good managerial interview test method to evaluate whether whom applicant has the best analysis effort in order to the managerial position, because they need to find the best solutions to give recommendations to attempt to solve any situational problems in any un predictive case study problems. For example, when the applicant or a focus group of discussion applicants whom need to spend the maximum half hours to give recommendations to discuss to solve one complex or difficult case study problem either between the interviewer and the another interviewee applicant or between the group of five to ten interviewees (job applicants) themselves. Thus, after the interviewer sent the one case study question to let the applicants to know by every email channel. The interviewer needs to judger whether whom one applicant or one of the focus group applicants their recommendations are the most reasonable to solve the case study managerial situational problem within half hour to one hour. Then, the interviewer can make more accurate judgement to select whether whom has the best analytical effort to do the managerial position.

3. The effectiveness of motivational interviewing for young or older adult applicants selection process

How can apply case management skills to be effective to prepare any interview motivation? How to do the most effective and efficient to meet the objectives of the interview? Some interview techniques used may vary the based on the individuals involved in the interview. For an interview with the young age applicant more require a different approach than an interview with a senior adult applicant. The following are one pointers to assist with preparing for the interview as below:

Knowing the purpose of the interview and what needs to be accomplished . What is the expected outcome? Gathering all forms that need to be completed or signed having the interview and making list of questions that need to be asked, knowing the key facts and topics to be discussed, during the interview. Gathering factual information that may be helpful. Opening mind is needed in the whole interview process. Making an appointment for the interview and arranging sufficient time to set fully participate in the interview. Taking notes during the interview, let the participants know in general terms the reason notes are being made and how they will be used, opening ended questions invite the applicant to provide more information usually begin with other words who, what, where, how, asking one question at a time and keeping wording simple and specific, defining any terms that may be unfamiliar to the applicant , giving the interviewing participants in the interview an opportunity to ask their one questions or to clarify anything that was discussed, closing the interview with a review of the information discussed and facts gathered, reviewing any follow-up that is to be done by the case manager or others involved in the interview.

In an efficient and effective interview, the interviewer needs have good body and spoken word communication to the interviewee or the position applicant. Because a good communication can reduce waste time or avoid the extended longer interview time if the interviewer can make good communication to impact good message to let the applicant to understand what is the mean to his/her interview question. What he/she wants to know, the total impact of a message includes ,e.g. 7 % verbal (words), 38% vocal /volume, pitch, rhythm etc. and 55% body movements (mostly facial expression). The interviewer's body and verbal behavior can make more clear message to let the interviewee(job applicant) to understand what answers are he/she wants to know mostly. Hence, an efficient and effective interview can let the interviewer to control and manage the whole interview to evaluate whether whom the applicants' answers or feedbacks are more reasonable to be acceptable to be better to compare other applicants to apply the position more accurately.

● What is efficient achievement of
technological inputs factor in
construction industry

What is organizational efficient raising actual mean? I shall indicate construction industry case to explain technological factor is the major factor to assist construction organization to raise efficiency. For construction industry example, improved productivity could be attributed to advances in and increased usage of information technologies, increased competition, due to globalization and changes in workplace and organizational structures.

For construction efficiency, the construction process can reduce waste in coordinating labor and in managing, moving and installing materials, loss avoidance. It can achieve efficient aim. The construction productive efficient concept can be defined efficiency improvements as ways to cut waste and labor. So, one construction organizational efficient achievement means that it implemented through the capital facilities sector, these activities would significantly advance construction efficiency and improve the quality, timeliness, cost effectiveness of projects in construction processes.

On construction industry technological factor influence hand, it can influence that construction productivity how well, how quality, and at what cost buildings and infrastructure can be constructured, directly affects prices for homes and consumer products and the robustness of the national economy. Construction productivity will also affect the outcomes of national efforts to renew existing infrastructure systems; to build new infrastructure for power from renewable to renew existing infrastructure systems; to build new infrastructure for power from renewable resources to develop high-performance " green building" and to remain competitive in the global market. If the construction organization expected to achieve effficient aim. It ought consider how to change in building design, construction and renovation and in building materials and materials recycling, will be essential to the success of national efforts to minimize environmental impacts, reduce overall energy use, and reduce greenhouse gas emissions.

However, construction industry analysts differ on whether construction industry productivity is improved by efficiency outcome. They indicate construction efficiency needs to reduce 25-50 percent waste in coordinating labour and in managing, moving and installing materials. This is the most minimum standard efficient achievement level to any construction organizations.

What are the factors influence efficiency to any construction organizations? An efficient construction task process is made possible by a range of information technological tools and applications, including computer-aided design and drafting, three and four dimensional visualization and modeling programs, laser scanning, cost-estimating and scheduling tools and materials tracking. So, high technological tool will assist to raise efficient construction process to any construction organizations. It can help them to shorten time and avoid materials waste and control cost effective estimation for any construction projects.

Effective use of interoperate technologies requires effective team cooperative processes and effective planning up front and this it can help overcome obstacles to efficiency created by process fragmentation. Interoperable technologies can also help to improve the quality and speed of any construction project related decision making, integrate processes, managing supply chains, sequence work flows, improve data accuracy and reduce the time spent on data entry, reduce design and engineering conflicts and the subsequent need for rework, improve the life-cycle management of buildings and infrastructure.

All of these factors will influence whether the construction organization can implement efficiency in success. For example, interoperable techcholgies include legal issues, data-storage capacities and the need for " intelligent " search applications to sort quickly through thousands of data elements and make real-time information available for on-site decision making. How to improve job-site efficiency through more effective interfacing of people, processes, materials ,equipment, and information. The job site for a large construction project is a dynamic place, involving numerous contractors, subcontractors, trades people and labors, all of whom must require equipment, materials and supplies to complete their tasks. So, they need to know how to manage activities and demands to achieve the maximum efficiency from the limited available resources. Time, money, and resources will have possible to be wasted when projects are poorly managed, causing workers to have to wait around for tools and work crews are not on-site at appropriate time or when supplies and equipment are stored in complexity or difficulty, requiring that they can be moved multiple time (time waste).

How to improve job site safety and improve the quality of projects, significantly cut waste? The use of automated equipment, e.g. for excavation and earthmoving operations, pip installation, concrete placement, and information technologies, e.g. radio-frequency identification tags for tracking materials personal digital assistants for capturing field data. These high technological tool can help any construction projects to raise efficiency to process improvements and the provision for real -time information for improved management at the job site.

Moreover, on mannal research and development tools hand, instead of data technological tools hand, any construction organizations also need to consider how to take a variety of forms: How to test field on a job site? How to arrange lecture shows in efficient way, seminrs, training and conference, and scientific laboratories time, human resource available arrangement, spending expenditure budget to finish. Moreover, effective performance mearements are enablers of innovation and of corrective actions throughout a construction project's life cycle. They can help any construction companies or organizations understand how processes led to success or failure, improvements or inefficiencies and how to use that knowledge to improve construction products , processes and outcomes of active projects.

The nature of construction projects, the industry itself, any construction organizations ought consider the construction working environment how to influence construction workers' emotions. For example, when the construction site is high levels, of noise, dust and airborne particles, adverse weather conditions,and other factors that can cause injuries and thereby reduce efficiency and productivity. New types of equipment can make an active physically easier to perform, easier to control, move precise , and safer for construction workers. Similarly, changes in materials can reduce the weight of construction components, make them easier to handle, move and install. Manufacturing building components off-site providers need more control conditions and allow for improved quality and precision in the fabrication of the component, One study that examined the relationship between changes in material technology and construction productivity based on 100 construction a related tasks, the study found that labor productivity for the same activity increased by 30 % at least when higher materials were used and labour productivity also improved when construction activites were performed using materials that were easier to install or were pre-fabricated. So, it seems material heavy can influence construction worker individual productive efficiency in site, if the material is higher , then the construction worker's productivity will be influenced to improve (Goodrum et al. 2009).

Thus, the factors influence construction organization's efficiency. It focuses on whether the construction firm applies how advanced construction technologies to assist its construction workers to work as well as whether its construction environment can let workers to feel safe to avoid life danger or accident occurrence. When the workers do not worry about whose life safety as well as they can apply advanced construction technology to assist them to work. Then, their productive efficiencies ought need to be improved easily. Thus, facility management and advanced technology will be the main factor to raise construction workers' efficiencies.

Reference

Barrick, M. R. & Mount , M.K. (1991). The big five personality dimensions and job performance: A meta-analysis, personnel psychology, 91, 1-26.

Costa, P.T. & Jr., & McCrae, R.R. (1992). Four ways five factors are basic. Personality and individual differences, 13, 653-665.

Gottredson, L.S. (Ed). (1982). The g factor in employment, Journal of vacational behavior, 29(3).

Hough, L.. (1992) The big five personality variables construct confusion: Description versus prediction human performance, 5, 135-155.

Hough, L.M. (1984). Development and evaluation of the " accomplishment record" methods of selecting and promoting professonals. Journal of applied psychology, 69, 135-146.

Hunter, J. (1986). Cognitive ability, cognitive aptitudes, job knowledge and job performance, Journal of vacational behavior, 29, 340-362.

Meichmann, D., Schmitt, N., & Harvey, V.S. (20010. Incremental validity of situatinal judgement tests , Journal of applied psychology, 86, 410-417.

Ree, M.J. Earles, J.A., & Teachout, M.S. (1994), Predicting job performance: Hot much more than g. Journal of applied psychology, 79, 518-524.

Robserton, I. T., & Smith, M. (2001). Personnel Selection. Journal Of Occupational And Organizational Psychological Psychology, 74(4), 441-472.

Sackett, P.R. & Wanek, J.E. (1996). New developments in the use of measures of honesty, integrity, conscientiousness, dependability, trustworthiness and reliability for personnel selection, personnel psychology, 49, 787-829.

Schuler, Randalls, S: Personnel and human resources management. Third edition, 1987.

Shoenfeldt, L.F. (1999). From dustbowl empiricism to rational constructs in biodata. Human resource management review, 9, 147-167.

Steven, Kay Cynthia (1997). Effects of pre-interview beliefs on applicant's reactions to campus interviews. Academy of management journal, 40(4), 947-966.

Stokes, G.S. Mumford, M.D. & owen, W.A. (Eds.) (1994). Biodata handbook paloacto, CA: CPP Books.

Thornton, G.C. III (1992). Assessment centers in human resources management Addison-Wesley,

Whetton, D.A. & Cameron, K.S. (2002). Developing Management , Skill 5th edition, reading, MA: Addison Wesley Longman.

www.ingramcontent.com/pod-product-compliance
Lightning Source LLC
Chambersburg PA
CBHW070907160726
48004CB00003B/1274